Kevin McCormack

Streets of London Buses

Capital Transport

First published 2021

ISBN 978 1 85414 454 6

Published by
Capital Transport Publishing Ltd
www.capitaltransport.com

Printed by Parksons Graphics

Front cover: RTs rule the road in this scene dating from 1971 on Albert Embankment just before the 170 was converted to OPO working with DMS buses on 24 July 1971. In the foreground RT 1082 is approaching Vauxhall Cross and would now be passing the Secret Intelligence Service (MI6) building which occupies the vacant ground on the left of the picture. Route 170 was introduced on 1 October 1950 to replace tram route 31 and was worked out of Wandsworth garage. The RT bearing fleet number 1082 was painted green from new until it received red livery in October 1965. The bus was sold for scrap in May 1974. (Fred Ivey)

Back cover upper: This photograph dating from early 1962 was taken from the Chiswick flyover which had opened in September 1959. The trolleybus in the foreground belongs to class L3 dating from 1939/40 and is on its way from Hammersmith to Hampton Court on route 667. The saplings on the roundabout have now grown into large trees and the buildings in the background have been redeveloped. (Phil Tatt/Online Transport Archive)

Back cover lower: The low point for the cross-London Green Line services was London Country's use of Leyland Nationals in the 1970s, a transformation subsequently taking place with the introduction of luxury coaches. SNC 178 crosses the famous London landmark of Westminster Bridge. (Capital Transport)

Title page: Overlooked by Tate & Lyle's sugar refinery out of view on the right, RM 1104 is on its way to Chingford station in August 1980 as it slows down to pick up a passenger in Albert Road, Beckton alongside the North London line to North Woolwich. All the buildings visible in this part of Albert Road have been replaced although the houses down the side streets such as Saville Road on the left remain. The distant cranes on the left of the picture are situated in the Royal Docks which have since become the site of London City Airport. Indeed, the 69 service, which had already been cut back from Chingford to Walthamstow on 19 November 1988, was diverted away from Silvertown and North Woolwich on 1 May 1999 to serve City Airport. However, it was withdrawn from the Airport to terminate at Canning Town station on 17 December 2005 as a result of the Docklands Light Railway (DLR) reaching the Airport a few days earlier. RM 1104 was re-registered 720 UXA in February 2004 and was withdrawn in the following November. It now resides in a Sussex garden centre. (Mike Russell)

INTRODUCTION

This colour album portrays London buses in a streetscape or landscape scenario and covers a period of some forty years from 1960 to the end of the 1990s. For the purposes of the book London is regarded as falling inside the London Boroughs but there are a few photographs outside the boundary showing routes which start within these boroughs.

As well as highlighting the buses and trolleybuses from the era the book features the surroundings such as buildings, cars and shop fronts as well as the fashions people wore. Most of these aspects have altered over the years as have, of course, the buses themselves. In most cases the captions of the pictures describe some of the changes to the scenes and also some history relating to the buildings etc, where appropriate. Reference is made to exact locations wherever possible to enable readers to view the scene today using Google Streetview.

The London Transport brand lasted from its inception in 1933 until responsibility was devolved to the Mayor of London in 2000 with the creation of Transport for London (TfL). For simplicity, the abbreviation LT is used throughout the period covered. Other abbreviations used are LGOC (London General Omnibus Company) which was LT's principal road transport predecessor and LCBS (London Country Bus Services) which assumed responsibility for LT's Country Bus and Green Line coach operations in 1970.

Finally, the abbreviation OPO (one person operation) is used throughout even though in earlier days OMO (one man operation) was the official term. Despite London's first conductress being employed as far back as 1915 (this was by Thomas Tilling on the joint LGOC/Tilling route 37), bus driving was long regarded as a male occupation as far as London buses was concerned until 1972 when LCBS employed its first female driver, with LT following suit two years later.

LS 489 and RM 795 proceed down Lambeth Palace Road alongside the Tudor gateway to Lambeth Palace (Morton's Tower) as they approach the roundabout adjacent to Lambeth Bridge in September 1982. Red Arrow route 507 (Victoria - Waterloo via Lambeth Bridge) commenced on 7 September 1968 with MBA Merlins and these were superseded by Leyland Nationals on 9 May 1981. LS 489 entered service in May 1981 and left London in January 1995 on transfer to Liverpool. Stamford Hill's RM 795 working a 149 service was withdrawn in November 1986 and sold, ultimately being preserved in the UK. The Palace of Westminster (Houses of Parliament) in its present incarnation as seen here was built mainly between 1840 and 1860 in Gothic Revival style. From this angle the Grade I Listed building is dominated by the Victoria Tower on the left. (Roy Marshall/The Bus Archive)

I must pay tribute now to two web sites which I have relied upon and which provide so much invaluable information to bus enthusiasts: Ian's Bus Stop for details of individual vehicles and Ian Armstrong's Bus Routes.

Several people have helped me compile this book. Firstly, I must thank the following individual photographers: Alan Murray, Bill Ryan, Alan Mortimer, John Ryan, Fred Ivey, Mike Russell, Chris Evans and Richard Franklin. I must also thank my fellow trustees at the Online Transport Archive: Charles Roberts, Peter Waller and Martin Jenkins. Assistance has also been provided by Matt Wharmby and, in addition, I must mention the London Bus Museum at Brooklands and James Whiting of Capital Transport, whose photographic collections have been made available to me. Finally, I wish to record the help provided by my grand-daughter, Marie Russell, who dealt with some of the computerised aspects of the task.

Kevin R McCormack
Ashtead, Surrey
September 2020

The tell-tale yellow posters attached to the traction poles indicate the imminent demise of trolleybus route 630 linking Scrubs Lane (near Willesden Junction) to West Croydon, the last day being 19 July 1960. This wet scene depicts Station Road, Croydon, where red trolleybuses could fraternise with green Country Area buses. Class K2 trolleybus No 1159 is about to pass Godstone-based RT 3126 working a short journey to Lingfield on the 409 to East Grinstead. This route, which was originally East Surrey's S9 service starting on 3 June 1922, still runs today to East Grinstead but from Selsdon which is located in the southern part of the London Borough of Croydon. It is operated by Southdown Buses. West Croydon bus station has seen several alterations over the years and the building on the left of this picture had to make way for the latest rebuild. The RT would now be standing at a tram stop. The buildings in the background, also in Station Road, remain in situ. (Phil Tatt/Online Transport Archive)

Opposite: AEC/MCW class L3 trolleybus No 1456 approaches the fork at Dawson's Corner, City Road, Shoreditch, in late October 1961, pursued by a Routemaster. A few days later (7 November) the 609 would run for the last time. Several trolleybus routes reached this point and some would take the right fork to East Road whereas the 609 would continue northwards along City Road (the Ring Road). The buildings on the left and right which are close to the Old Street roundabout still exist but Dawson's huge department store has been replaced by an enormous skyscraper. The shop is remembered for having a talking caged parrot on the ground floor and after every annual Boat Race would hoist up a dark blue or light blue flag above the main entrance, depending on whether Oxford or Cambridge won! (John Ryan)

Above: Trolleybus 1500 looks immaculate in this c.1960 view as it makes its way from North Finchley along Grays Inn Road, at the Kings Cross station end. The 621 was introduced on 6 March 1938 to replace tram route 21 and succumbed to replacement by a new motor bus route, the 221, from 8 November 1961. For much of its 31-year existence (1931-1962) the London trolleybus system was the largest in the world and at its peak operated 68 routes and 1811 vehicles. The two dominant buildings in this picture have survived. On the extreme right is the former family home of the Willing family whose business was advertising. This Grade II Listed building, designed in the French baroque style, dates from 1909 and is now a Travelodge. The building behind the trolleybus is now devoid of its advertising hoarding and at the rear of 1500 is the former Kings Cross Cinema (later called the Scala) which opened in 1920 and remains an entertainment venue. (Vic Goldberg/courtesy LCC Tramways Trust)

Hampstead Road looks busy in this photograph taken in April 1961 shortly before the bus replacement on 26 April of both trolleybus routes seen here. The vehicles are K1 No 1057 and K2 No 1170, both all-Leyland products from 1938/9. Each will be terminating at Tottenham Court Road, the 629 having come from Enfield and the 627 from Waltham Cross. All the buildings visible have been demolished apart from the one with all the chimney pots behind the roof of 1057. This is the former St Pancras Female Orphanage rebuilt in 1904 and now a medical centre (St James House, 110 Hampstead Road). The tall building beyond has recently been demolished in connection with the construction of the HS2 railway line from Euston. This is the former National Temperance Hospital which occupied a large site and included the building with the pointed roof. (John Ryan)

RM 36 displays its early bodywork (non-opening front upstairs windows) and original radiator grille (no AEC triangle) in this view at Ludgate Circus while working a 48 service from North Woolwich to Waterloo in late 1961. At the time the bus was based at Poplar, its home for two years from November 1959. The route number 48 had four iterations, this one being the third, and lasted for some six years. The service was withdrawn on 27 January 1965, being replaced by the 40A and 40B. The bridge bearing the Coat of Arms of the City of London and carrying trains from Blackfriars to Holborn Viaduct was removed in 1990 as a result of the sub-surface St Paul's/City Thameslink station being built and the re-opening of the Snow Hill tunnel. The King Lud pub dates from 1870 and closed in 2005 but the facade remains in place today. (Fred Ivey)

This busy 1962 winter scene in Euston Road, at the junction with Upper Woburn Place, has plenty of FX3 taxis visible but none of the successor FX4s which entered production in 1958. From February 1958 to April 1962 the bus in the foreground, RTL 704, was based at Stockwell garage which provided some buses for the service seen here, the 77A from Kings Cross to Raynes Park. This was a time when RTs and RTLs shared this route until RTs took over completely on 6 March 1967. Meanwhile, RTL 704 had been withdrawn in November 1966 and exported to Ceylon (Sri Lanka). RMs succeeded RTs on this service from 15 December 1973. Route 77A first reached Raynes Park in February 1924 but was renumbered 177 later that year before reverting to 77A in October 1934. It was renumbered 87 on 3 June 2006, by which time it had become the last suffix-numbered service. All the buildings visible have been replaced but the posts on the far left forming part of a brick wall are still extant as they belong to Euston Fire Station, a Grade II* listed building which is just out of view. (Ian Stewart/Online Transport Archive)

It is the last day of trolleybus route 647 (Stamford Hill – London Docks), 18 July 1961, and the usual yellow announcement of the conversion to buses is affixed to the stop. Making its way to Stamford Hill is No 1326 from the all-Leyland K2 class introduced in 1939. The vehicle is in Dock Road, Whitechapel, heading for Leman Street and onwards past No 99, the magnificent former Co-operative Wholesale Company London Branch Headquarters with clock tower. This Grade II Listed building, now known as Sugar House, was opened in 1887 and has since been converted into flats. Also surviving today is the building on the extreme left, 66 Royal Mint Street, which was built in 1890 as a tobacco factory and later became a warehouse. In front of the bridge carrying the Fenchurch Street railway line another bridge has since been added which enables the Docklands Light Railway to reach Tower Gateway station. This has resulted in the removal of Trafalgar House. The buildings behind the bridge apart from Sugar House have also been replaced. (John Ryan)

The trolleybus wires have been removed in High Road, Willesden, as RM 1007 meets a Commer van on its journey from Hammersmith to Edgware station in May 1962. The 266 was introduced on 3 January 1962 to replace trolleybus route 666 and still runs today, but terminates at Brent Cross instead of Edgware. The bus, based at Stonebridge Park from its entry into service in January 1962 until July 1962, is displaying the route number in the offside aperture, a practice which was soon discontinued apparently to deter potential passengers from running across the road. RM 1007 remained in service until January 1991 and was then scrapped. Crew-operated Ms replaced RMs on the 266 on 2 February 1985 and the service became OPO nine months later. This scene is largely unchanged today apart from the replacement of the London Co-operative Service (LCS) building on the left by Utopia House. The row of chimney pots at 164 High Road remains in place as does the former Willesden Green Primitive Methodist Chapel with copula in the background which is still a church. (Fred Ivey)

Opposite upper: In this 1962 scene the centre of Twickenham is dominated by Barclays Bank and that remains the case today. Indeed the only significant change to this particular townscape has been the removal of the trolleybus wires and traction poles. Barclays Bank is a Grade II Listed early Edwardian edifice designed in Italianate style and is positioned between York Street on the left and Church Street located behind the trolleybuses. The front vehicle is No 1518 which is operating a 605 service to Teddington and Wimbledon. Abandonment is imminent because there is a yellow notice attached to the bus stop. Interestingly, it was at this very stop that two decorated trolleybuses began London's inaugural trolleybus run to Teddington on 16 May 1931, replacing tram route 69 between these points. This pioneering trolleybus service and those which followed later in 1931 on delivery of more trolleybuses was introduced by London United Tramways, two years before the company was absorbed into LT. (Phil Tatt/Online Transport Archive)

Opposite: AEC/MCW L3 trolleybus No 1444 stands at the Wimbledon terminus of route 604 from Hampton Court shortly before the final conversion to motor buses. The location is the junction of Wimbledon Bridge and Queen's Road and all the buildings still exist. The Town Hall dating from 1931 has become a supermarket but the clock is still in place, as are the lamps beside the portico. However, the ornamental lamps and unique road signs, as well as the underground toilet surrounded by railings, have been removed. Route TB4 was a new trolleybus route introduced in 1931 with vehicles operating from the former tram depot at Fulwell and was renumbered 604 in 1935. Fulwell depot, along with Isleworth, was also the last to use trolleybuses. The final day for the 604 and the other six services from those depots was 8 May 1962. (Online Transport Archive)

In an unchanged scene on Victoria Embankment (apart from the vehicle), RFW 14 collects passengers outside Embankment tube station in the 1950s. The fleet of fifteen 8 ft wide Regal IV RFW coaches with Eastern Coachworks bodies were ordered by LT, along with 25 RF sightseeing coaches, to enhance the Private Hire fleet for the Festival of Britain which opened on the South Bank on 4 May 1951. The coach was one of four lasting with LT through the 1964 summer season before being withdrawn and is one of two, the other being RFW 6, to be preserved. The Portland stone tube station building was built in 1914, replacing an earlier brick structure. In the background a Southern electric train can be seen on Hungerford railway bridge adjoining Charing Cross station. (Capital Transport)

Route 11 is not alone in often being regarded as a cheap means of sightseeing since it passes many famous landmarks between Liverpool Street and Fulham Broadway. It is also one of the earliest routes, starting in 1906, although its western terminus has changed over the years, having previously reached Shepherds Bush and Hammersmith. RTWs were introduced on route 11 on 2 May 1951 and were succeeded by RMs from 1 February 1966. This example, RTW 252, was withdrawn in September 1965 and exported to Ceylon (Sri Lanka). The last ones were retired from public service on 14 May 1966 but some continued on training duties until 1970 as they were the same width as RMs (8ft). This shot taken in Whitehall dates from August 1963. The National Gallery is visible in the distance. Behind the bus on the corner of Great Scotland Yard is The Clarence pub dating from 1862. (W Ryan)

Left: For several years Poplar garage provided a special dock service for the Port of London Authority (PLA) carrying dock workers within the Royal group of docks. This view from July 1963 depicts RTL 817 at Royal Victoria Dock (Custom House) bound for Manor Way in King George V Docks. Behind the bus is the Hornby Grange, a refrigerated cargo ship built in 1946 and broken up in 1972. RTL 817 was withdrawn in July 1966 and shipped to Ceylon (Sri Lanka). (Edward Shepherd/London Bus Museum)

Opposite top: With a backdrop consisting of South Africa House (completed in 1933) and, on the right, a parade of shops and offices which has been rebuilt sympathetically and is much improved, RT 2708 leaves Trafalgar Square, heading into Whitehall, in August 1963. The bus is carrying a Park Royal roof box body and was withdrawn in September 1964, followed by exportation to Ceylon (Sri Lanka). Route 12's north western terminus at this time was Willesden Junction. It is now Oxford Circus but the service still goes to Dulwich. Route 12 started under the General's auspices in 1908 running between Turnham Green and Ilford but by 1911 this latter terminus had been changed to Peckham and the service was jointly operated by LGOC and Tilling in order to stave off competition from the National Steam Car Company. Also in 1911 Tilling introduced hybrid buses (so not a new invention today!) on the 12 in the form of Tilling-Stevens petrol-electric vehicles. (W Ryan)

Above: A long line of buses occupy the Archway station stand at the foot of Highgate Hill in October 1964. In the foreground working a 137 service is brand new RM 2022 based at Gillingham Street (Victoria) garage. This bus enjoyed a long career in London and following withdrawal in January 2005 it was exported to Spain. Next in line is RT 3355 also operating on route 137 and displaying an old upper case front blind. Route 137 originally ran from Archway to West Wickham when it was introduced on 3 October 1934 as a renumbered version of the 536. Behind the RT is a 27 service in the hands of an RTL. There has been some recent redevelopment on this part of Highgate Hill but the building with the prominent dome is still standing although obscured by trees from this viewpoint. It is St Joseph's church dating from 1889. (Fred Ivey)

Camberwell-based RTL 899 meets another RTL crossing Tower Bridge in March 1965. Route 42 (currently running from Liverpool Street-East Dulwich) has undergone several small route changes over the years as well as seeing a variety of vehicle types. RTLs were replaced by RTs on 16 May 1966 and the service became OPO on 24 January 1970, fluctuating between single and double deck operation. On 7 February 1987 more radical change occurred when green single deckers (Leyland Nationals) arrived owned by London Country South East. This morphed into Kentish Bus & Coach and the buses then became maroon and cream. The service is now operated by normal red double deckers. The structures in this picture need no introduction. Tower Bridge was completed in 1894 but the Tower of London in the background is very much older, most of it dating from the period 1078-1285. (W Ryan)

Carrying upper case blinds and photographed around 1965, RM 824 stands outside the Queen Anne style Edwardian buildings which dominate this end of Stamford Hill. The distinctive red brick parade with Portland stone dressings is still intact, as is the parade in the background. The bus carrying fleet number RM 834 spent many years at Stamford Hill garage (from October 1961 to July 1970) and was withdrawn in May 1986. It was then sold to Kelvin Scottish and re-registered TSK 271 in 1992. Route 67 (London Docks – Northumberland Park station) was a trolleybus replacement service for the 647 and was introduced on 19 July 1961 using RMs from the outset. The next ten years saw the service operated by Leyland Atlanteans (XAs), green Daimler Fleetlines (XFs) and RMLs before OPO DMS vehicles took over on 4 December 1971. (John Herting/Online Transport Archive)

RTL 1294 turns out of Mitcham Lane into Southcroft Lane on the Streatham/Tooting border in November 1965. The 181 between Streatham and Victoria was introduced on 14 May 1952 as a renumbering of the previous 57A service and was RTL-operated from the outset, initially from Clapham garage and then from Stockwell. The route became OPO on 2 January 1971 with SMS buses replacing RMs. DMSs were in charge when the service ran for the last time on 24 April 1981. Back in 1968, RTL 1294 joined several of its classmates on a one-way journey to Ceylon (Sri Lanka). The location in this picture has hardly changed over the years. The pedestrian crossing has not been moved but the shop fascias have altered with changes of ownership and there are no longer any canopy blinds (retractable awnings) in evidence. In LCC tram days Southcroft Lane was referred to by locals as "the prairie" because of the open nature of the surrounding land. (Alan Mortimer)

This picture taken on Blackfriars Bridge in November 1965 is dominated by the Grade II Listed Unilever House which was completed in 1933 for the soap manufacturer, Lever Brothers. The bridge, which replaced an earlier one, was opened in 1869 and widened in 1907-09 to accommodate tramlines. The photographer has used one of the viewing parapets which overhang the river to film RTW 387. Route 45 originated on 1 October 1950 following the abandonment of the 34 tram service and then replaced trolleybus routes 513/613 on 1 February 1961 when the terminus was moved from Farringdon Street to Hampstead Heath. The other end of the route was South Kensington Station, the destination to which RTW 387 is heading by means of a circuitous route via Brixton and Camberwell and re-crossing the Thames over Battersea Bridge. RTWs replaced RTLs on the 45 on 26 November 1958 and RMs took over the service entirely from 23 January 1966, having previously only operated on Sundays. A month later RTW 387 was sold to a local coach company. (Alan Mortimer)

Above: This picture was taken on the last day of RTW operation in public service (14 May 1966) and the example seen here, RTW 467 (since preserved), had the honour of making the final run, returning to Brixton garage in the early hours of the following morning. Route 95 (Cannon Street-Tooting) was a replacement for tram service 10 and started on 7 January 1951 with RTs. These were replaced by RTWs on 1 October 1963 but their tenure lasted less than three years. They were succeeded by RMs which in turn were superseded by OPO DMS buses on 2 January 1971. The route was withdrawn on 1 February 1991. The RTW is parked outside the entrance to Brixton garage located in Streatham Hill opposite Telford Avenue. The bus garage which is still in use was built in 1951 on the site of the former Telford Avenue tram depot. Saunders-bodied RT 4656 from Streatham garage on route 159 has crept into the picture on the left and behind stands the renowned apartment block known as Pullman Court which is Grade II* Listed and dates from 1933-5. (Capital Transport)

Opposite: An innovation for London occurred on 18 April 1966 when the first flat-fare Red Arrow express service, the 500, operating between Victoria and Marble Arch/Oxford Circus, was introduced. Six Strachans-bodied AEC Merlins with twenty-five seats and provision for forty-eight standing passengers entered service to operate this pioneer route. Following its success, a further seven Red Arrow routes were added from 7 September 1968 which saw the arrival of the more familiar MCW-bodied Merlins and caused the fifteen Strachans bodied Merlins of the XMA and Country Area XMB classes mostly to have short operating lives. XMA 6, seen here in Park Lane in September 1966, was withdrawn in August 1973 having spent most of the previous four years in store and was sold to a buyer in the Irish Republic but was blown up in January 1978. In the foreground of this picture is an Aston Martin which may have emerged from the underground car park on the right. The building in the background on the left is the J W Marriott Grosvenor House Hotel which opened in 1929 on the site of Grosvenor House, the residence of the Dukes of Westminster (the Grosvenor family). (Roy Marshall)

Route 271 (Highgate Village – Moorgate (Finsbury Square) started on 20 July 1960, replacing trolleybus route 611, and maintains the same routeing today. Leyland Atlantean XAs replaced RMs on this service on 1 December 1965 as part of the comparative trials between RMLs, Daimler Fleetline XFs and XAs. RMLs took over the service on 10 July 1966. XA 12, seen here in May 1966, was withdrawn in February 1973 and all fifty of this type were exported to Hong Kong. In this view the bus is travelling along Holloway Road against the backdrop of the Jones Brothers department store. Latterly, this belonged to the John Lewis Partnership and extended all the way to the ABC cinema seen behind the bus. The store closed in 1990 and a new Waitrose supermarket of retrospective appearance has replaced the lower level section. The large ornate building remains in place, converted into offices. The ABC cinema which opened in 1940 as the Savoy cinema has been tastefully converted into a pub called The Coronet which was the cinema's name when it closed in 1983. (Alan Mortimer)

LT incurred serious staffing problems in the early 1960s and decided to abolish its private hire fleet. Instead, non-core activities were outsourced, including the Round Tour, a two-hour sightseeing experience starting in Buckingham Palace Road alongside Victoria railway station, as seen here in August 1966 (the Tour was renamed the Round London Sightseeing Tour in 1968). Samuelsons was ideally positioned to provide the transport as its garage was located adjacent to Victoria Coach station which was also in Buckingham Palace Road. The coach in the picture is a Samuelson Dragonfly, one of only six Duple (Northern)-bodied centre-entrance AEC Reliance 4U3As built, four of which were for Samuelsons and delivered in 1963. On the right of the coach is the side of the Grosvenor Hotel. The old building on the left has been replaced. (W Ryan)

This view of RT 1236 in May 1967 shows the most obvious distinguishing feature of a Saunders body: the rearwards positioning of the offside route number panel. LT purchased 300 of these well-made and robust bodies and this vehicle is from the first batch of 250. By coincidence, at its final overhaul in January 1966 at Aldenham Works when almost any type of body could have been fitted, it received another Saunders body, albeit not its original one. Consequently, the bus was able to retain its authentic appearance until its withdrawal in May 1969 and subsequent scrapping. In this photograph, RT 1236 is operating on route 244 which was originally a single deck route until RTs were introduced on 6 May 1953. OPO SMS vehicles took over on 16 January 1971 and the service was withdrawn on 24 April 1982. Buses still terminate at this bus stand in the centre of Muswell Hill Broadway encircled by magnificent early Edwardian shopping parades. The road disappearing into the distance is Dukes Avenue and the spire protruding above the shops belongs to the Baptist church. (Capital Transport)

The last RTL routes were the 176 and 226 operating from Willesden garage, the final day of scheduled service being 29 November 1968. This example, RTL 1338, was one of thirteen still licensed on the final day and was then withdrawn. After being stripped for spares which were sent to Ceylon to help maintain the RTLs previously dispatched to that country, the remains were scrapped in the UK. This photograph was taken in Waterloo Road in October 1967, with the bus passing the headquarters and major supermarket premises of David Greig. This now largely forgotten family retailer had over 220 food stores in the 1960s, mainly in southern England, before significant death duties forced the company to be sold. The building seen here, Scotch House, 145 Waterloo Road, was completed in 1928. It was demolished in the late 1970s and replaced by a government building, Wellington House, but the impressive facade, based on Selfridges in Oxford Street, has been preserved. Behind the bus is the side of the Old Vic Theatre which opened in 1818 and had its interior rebuilt in 1871 when it was known as the Royal Victoria Palace. (Alan Mortimer)

In addition to RTL 1507 everything in this view from October 1967 in Burdett Road, Mile End, near the junction with Ackroyd Drive, has vanished: the shops (now replaced by a grassed area), the pub visible through the arch (The Victoria Hotel), even the railway bridge which was reconstructed in 1984 to allow for road widening. The only surviving elements are the overhead electric railway gantry and the tower block with the roof-mounted structure. Until its closure in 1941 Burdett Road railway station on the Fenchurch Street – Shoeburyness line was located here but was not well patronised as prospective passengers tended to use nearby Mile End Underground station. When this picture was taken, route 106 went from Finsbury Park to Becontree, so RTL 1507 is working a short journey to Poplar (Blackwall Tunnel). This became the terminus from 16 January 1971 when the route was shortened. Interestingly, the arched railway bridge was signposted as having a 14ft height limitation, yet the 677 trolleybus service could pass under it, even with overhead wires in place! (Alan Mortimer)

Against the backdrop of Greenwich gasworks Catford-based RT 1311 emerges from the 108B terminus in Boord Street to enter Tunnel Avenue in March 1968. This route did not pass though Blackwall Tunnel and was introduced on 12 October 1960 to provide an improved Monday-Friday service south of the river. RTs were replaced by OPO SMs on 17 April 1971 and after some routeing changes the service was withdrawn on 9 November 1991. Meanwhile RT 1311 expired in April 1973 and was sold for scrap. Today, this location is recognisable only by the framework surrounding the large gas holder which is still extant. Tunnel Avenue is a dual carriageway, Boord Street has been re-aligned and the mock-Tudor Mitre Arms pub, which latterly was incorporated into a music and entertainment venue called Studio 338 (which still exists), burnt down in 2016. Some of the yellow support towers belonging to the O2 Arena (formerly the Millennium Dome) can now be seen behind the site of the smaller gas holder. (Edward Shepherd/London Bus Museum)

Route 118 was introduced on 18 November 1936 to run between Clapham Common and Mitcham Common, replacing a withdrawn section of the 5. This view dates from May 1968 and depicts RT 3572 in Greyhound Lane at its junction with Streatham High Road (A3) opposite Streatham Common. In the 1970s RTs gradually gave way to RMs on the 118 with total replacement occurring on 23 May 1976. OPO Ms took over on 27 April 1985. RT 3572 spent nearly ten years (March 1964 – October 1973) at Streatham garage, after which it was withdrawn and exported to California. This scene is relatively unchanged today but the horse trough has been removed. The Greyhound pub, in its rebuilt 1930 manifestation, is now the Rabbit Hole and its facade is festooned with painted rabbits. The building on the right also survives in an altered state. (Edward Shepherd/London Bus Museum)

The penultimate RLH route was the 248 from Upminster to Cranham which has since been re-routed away from the low bridge in St Mary's Lane, Cranham, to allow standard height double deckers to be used. Ironically, the service was OPO way back in the early 1930s when a Dennis Dart (first generation!) was used until crew operation was introduced in 1936. The 248 then became OPO again on 19 September 1970 when SMSs replaced the RLHs. This view in Upminster in May 1968 depicts RLH 73 pulling out of Station Road into St Mary's Lane against a backdrop which is largely unaltered today apart from the inevitable change of retailers and the removal of the wall-mounted clock. RLH 73 was based at Hornchurch garage, coded RD because from its construction in 1924 until 1935 it was called Romford garage. RLH 73 was withdrawn in September 1970 and exported to Germany. (W Ryan)

The man puffing on his pipe will have to wait a little longer for a bus because the stop only serves routes 114 and 158, not the 140 or 183. This photograph taken in May 1968 in Station Road, Harrow depicts a town centre "old style" Sunday when Sunday trading was very limited. That it is a Sunday is also confirmed by the presence of RM 2197 on the 183 which was RT-operated every day except Sundays until 4 January 1975 when total conversion of the route to OPO DMS occurred. The 140 survived with RTs until 15 July 1978 when RMs took over and significant change occurred on 23 April 1983 when OPO was introduced and the service cut back from Mill Hill to Harrow Weald garage. Since 7 December 2019 the route no longer serves Heathrow Airport but terminates in Hayes. All the buildings seen here are still standing and the bank on the left (now rebranded NatWest) at 315 Station Road is still open. However, the section of St Anne's Road behind the RT has been pedestrianised. (Capital Transport)

As it travels northwards along Kings Road, Chelsea, in May 1968, Holloway's RT 2830 seems to have caught the attention of both a Chelsea Pensioner standing on the corner of Wellington Square and a dog at the entrance to Bywater Street. Route 19's origin can be traced back to the London Road Car Company's service J (Clapham Junction to Highbury Barn) which began in 1906 and was numbered 19 in 1908. However, when pictured here it operated from Finsbury Park to Tooting Bec. RMs gradually replaced RTs and took over completely from 12 August 1972. Some Routemasters continued to operate

this service until it was converted to double deck OPO on 2 April 2005. RT 2830 remained in service until February 1974 and was sold for scrap in the following year. This location is unchanged today apart from different retailers occupying the shops. The Chelsea Pensioner, who is carrying a tray of flags and holding a donation box, is wearing his scarlet uniform, a requirement in public places for former soldiers living at the retirement and nursing home known as the Royal Hospital, Chelsea. (W Ryan)

Pulling in to the bus stop to pick up eager passengers RM 1893 heads a line of buses travelling northwards along Kings Road, Chelsea in May 1968. The two buses immediately behind the RM are RTs operating on route 19. RM 1893, allocated at this time to Battersea garage, was withdrawn in August 1984 and sold for scrap. Route 22, which originated in 1909 initially running between Clapton and Elephant & Castle and then Homerton to Putney, had latterly been operated by RTLs until replaced by RTs and RMs on 1 October 1967 and was worked exclusively by RMs from 11 November 1967. The 22 was truncated to operate only between Putney Common and Piccadilly Circus from 24 February 1990 and the Monday-Saturday service became OPO on 22 July 2005 when the RMLs were replaced. Sunday services had been OPO since 7 February 1987. There have been no significant changes to this part of Kings Road over the years apart from the replacement of the petrol filling station on the corner of Walpole Street, seen on the extreme left. (W Ryan)

Four taxis and three buses monopolise the busy Strand in late May 1968. One of the taxis is turning into Savoy Court to reach the hotel. On the left is the Strand Palace Hotel dating from 1909 and on the right, evidenced by the canopy, is Simpson's, a restaurant which opened in 1828. In the distance is St Mary le Strand church which was consecrated in 1723. The central lamp standards remain in place today but the gas lamp in the foreground has been removed although an identical one stands some fifty yards behind the photographer. There are some 1,500 gas lamps remaining in London, protected by English Heritage. Route 60 started on 11 October 1961 as a renumbering of the 260. The northern terminus was extended from Colindale to Cricklewood on 27 January 1965 when it was also cut back from Surrey Docks to Waterloo. The service was withdrawn on 7 September 1968 while still operated by RTLs such as this example, RTL 1502. The Cricklewood- Oxford Circus section became the 8B and Red Arrow route 505 covered the Oxford Circus – Waterloo part. (W Ryan)

Route 242 just managed to squeeze onto the Central Area bus map for this period (June 1968), running along the top edge eastwards between South Mimms and Epping Forest. This service had been operated by single deckers until RTs replaced Leyland Tigers (TDs) on 6 May 1953. RTs from Potters Bar garage then reigned until 30 November 1968 when OPO Merlins took over. The vehicle in this picture, RT 2881, was withdrawn in October 1970 and followed the route that most of its contemporaries and later types took to a well known Yorkshire scrapyard. The bus has just climbed Judges Hill in the village of Northhaw and has reached the junction of Northaw Road West and Vineyards Road. In the background is St Thomas a Becket church, built in 1881. This scene has not changed significantly over the years. (Roy Marshall/The Bus Archive)

Crowds descend on Battersea Park to watch the Royal Tournament parade on 23 June 1968. Dolly stops have been placed in the Park for the shuttle buses running between Sloane Square and Battersea Pleasure Gardens (as described on the bus blinds). In 1968, the Tournament, which was the largest and oldest military tattoo and pageant in the world, opened at Earls Court on 1 July, the Battersea Park armed forces parade being a popular curtain raiser to the actual event. The Royal Tournament took place annually from 1880 until 1999. The 137A special service seen here is operated by Norwood-based RM 1020. This vehicle remained in service until April 1993 and was then sold to Bluebird Bus & Coach of Middleton, Manchester. A St John's Ambulance is parked on the opposite side of the road. (W Ryan)

Fresh from overhaul at Aldenham, RT 4083 turns out of The Ridgeway, Enfield, and into the former Chase Farm Hospital in June 1968 on a 128 service from Lower Edmonton. This was originally single deck route 204 and was converted to double deck and renumbered 128 on 13 August 1941. The 128 operated until 14 June 1969 and was then replaced by new route W8. RT 4083 was withdrawn in June 1973 and sold for scrap. A new Chase Farm Hospital next to the old one opened in 2018 and the former site is being redeveloped for residential and educational use. However, the clock tower building with pinnacle is due to be retained. This was built in 1886 as an orphanage and later an old people's home before becoming Chase Farm Hospital. (John Herting/Online Transport Archive)

Also seen on 23 June 1968 is RM 2087 as it sets off on the Battersea Park to Sloane Square shuttle service. The bus, which was withdrawn in February 1987 and eventually exported to Hungary, is pictured on Chelsea Bridge, a relatively modern Thames crossing dating from 1934-7 and replacing an earlier structure. This vista is unchanged today, even down to the lamps on the bridge. The brick building in the distance is the private Lister Hospital occupying premises completed in 1898. On the right, with oval louvres in the roof, is the Western Pumping Station and associated chimney located in Grosvenor Road, dating from 1875. (W Ryan)

Two young ladies smile at the camera at Richmond station on a wet day in July 1968 as the photographer composes his shot of RT 1200 to include the pre-nationalisation station sign. This features two companies (the original Southern Railway and the London, Midland and Scottish Railway (LMS)) which both ceased to exist twenty years earlier. The latter company operated the Broad Street-Richmond electrified service. Route 65A had a short and rather complex existence replacing or supplementing parts of the 65 service (Ealing (Argyle Road) to Leatherhead), sometimes only on certain days. It operated from 11 October 1950 to 14 May 1952 until replaced by new route 265 and then from 9 October 1963 to 30 November 1968 until renumbered 65. On that last date route 71 was extended to cover the southernmost sections of the 65 and 65A. RT 1200 was allocated to Kingston garage from April 1966 to October 1973 and remained in service until October 1977, followed by disposal for scrapping. (W Ryan)

Having just passed Mile End underground station RTL 1619 heads south along Mile End Road towards the junction with Burdett Road on its journey to the route 10 terminus at Victoria station. RTs replaced RTLs on Mondays to Saturdays from 7 September 1968, with Sunday workings already being operated by RMs. All the commercial properties seen here, including the Odeon Cinema, have been demolished except the white building at the rear of the bus on the corner of Rhondda Grove. Over the years route 10 has had a variety of northern termini such as Woodford Bridge, Chigwell and Abridge until its withdrawal on 16 January 1988. The number was first used by the Vanguard Motor Bus Company in 1907 when the service ran between Elephant & Castle and Clapton and became LGOC route 10 when Vanguard merged with LGOC in the following year, by which time it was running between Elephant and Leytonstone. (John Herting/Online Transport Archive)

Against the backdrop of an unrecognisable scene in Poplar today, RTL 1418 prepares to take the southbound bore of the Blackwall Tunnel on 18 August 1968 on its journey from Bromley-by-Bow to Crystal Palace. The tunnel was opened in 1897 and Thomas Tilling immediately introduced a horse bus service between Poplar and Greenwich which was replaced in 1912 by a motor bus service (route 69) operated by LGOC and renumbered 108 in March 1914. Because of the shape of the tunnel bore and the numerous bends, double deck buses used on the 108 required special domed roofs (latterly the 40 tunnel STLs introduced in 1937) and reinforced tyres but when the road level was altered in 1953 LT was able to operate standard height RTLs. These were briefly replaced by RTs on 7 September 1968. A new bore without a height restriction had been opened in 1967 for southbound traffic and the original tunnel was subsequently modified for northbound traffic. However, the alterations included raising the road level to widen the carriageway, creating a height restriction which prevented further use of double deckers. OPO Merlins therefore took over the 108 from 26 October 1968. Both ends of the original tunnel were marked by ornate arched gate houses. Only the southern one survives and is Grade II Listed. (W Ryan)

Green Line route 719 was a late joiner to the network, starting on 11 July 1956 and operating between Hemel Hempstead and Victoria, with vehicles supplied by Garston garage. RMCs replaced RFs on this service in November 1962 and conversion to OPO took place on 23 November 1968, ironically using RFs, on which date the route was extended to Wrotham to cover withdrawn route 717. This picture of RMC 1512 at the Marble Arch roundabout was taken in late November 1967 during the vehicle's brief allocation to Garston for a few weeks around that time. The coach was purchased by LT in March 1980 and sold for scrap in October 1992. The buildings in the background on the left are in Oxford Street and the remainder are in Park Lane. The triumphal arch giving its name to the area is visible behind the large tree. It was completed in 1833 and erected in the courtyard of Buckingham Palace before being moved to its present location in 1851 when the present facade of the palace was constructed. The arch was then intended to be a ceremonial entrance to Hyde Park (on the right of the picture) but road alterations have left it marooned on a large traffic island. (John Herting/Online Transport Archive)

The date is Sunday 1 September 1968 and Windsor garage has prepared for an influx of tourists visiting Windsor over the bank holiday weekend by providing RML buses to operate Green Line relief coach services. The location is the open air Green Line Coach Station on Eccleston Bridge situated above the platforms of Victoria railway station. RML 2447 appears to have arrived on a short working of the 718 (Windsor to Harlow) and is being overtaken by RML 2454 which is destined to work a short on the 704 (Tunbridge Wells to Windsor) service. Both buses were later purchased by LT and painted red, remaining in service until 2004 when they were sold. RML 2454 is now available for wedding hire. The Bishops building has since been demolished. (W Ryan)

This is Finborough Road, SW10, at the junction with Ifield Road and Redcliffe Square in September 1968. Although the junction has since been altered and trees planted in the middle, all the buildings remain, including the Finborough Arms pub in the centre, built in 1868. Battersea-based RT 2555 was withdrawn in November 1971 and sold for scrap and all the other vehicles in this picture have almost certainly suffered the same fate, with one notable exception: the 1929 Austin 12/4 Burnham saloon car (GC 2479) on the right which was sold at auction in 2013 for £7,600 and is currently licensed. The bus is heading north towards the junction with Old Brompton Road on its journey from Chelsea to Camden Town. Route 31 still runs but its routeing has changed over the years. In 1911 it ran from South Hampstead to Chelsea. Now the service operates between White City and Camden Town and no longer frequents Finborough Road. (W. Ryan)

Opposite: In the first view a British European Airways (BEA) front-entrance Routemaster (NMY 653E) followed by a conventional one on route 74 stand in West Cromwell Road at the junction with Earls Court Road in September 1968. The BEA vehicle was delivered in February 1967 and, following the cessation of airline check-in facilities at the West London Air Terminal in 1974, became surplus to requirements. It was purchased by LT in November 1976 and designated RMA 25. LT eventually purchased all 65 of these vehicles and used most of them as staff buses. In October 1994, RMA 25 was sold and exported to Ireland. This narrow section of Cromwell Road has since been widened and turned into a dual carriageway. In the lower view in the same month, NMY 649E waits in Cromwell Road ready to cross Warwick Road, Earls Court, on its way from Heathrow Airport to the West London Air Terminal. By coincidence it has pulled up behind a British Overseas Airways Corporation (BOAC) Duple-bodied Ford Thames Mariner coach, FYF 254C, delivered in July 1965, and belonging to a fleet of 14 such vehicles. This may be heading to BOAC's London air terminal in Victoria. The two nationalised airlines (BEA and BOAC), along with two regional airlines (Cambrian and Northeast), were merged into newly formed British Airways (BA) in 1974. The West London Air Terminal closed in March 1979 by which time the BA fleet of Routemasters had already been significantly reduced. A large building which includes a Tesco supermarket now stands on the vacant land behind the vehicles. The low level houses are still in situ. (W Ryan)

Above: It is approaching midnight but not only is this the last 82 service of the day (25 October 1968) it is also the last service bus to pass through Rotherhithe Tunnel for another twenty years and the last-ever double decker. It is too dark to see the reinforced front tyres on Poplar's RT 1674 to protect against kerb rubbing due to the narrowness of the tunnel. The bus is standing at a location which no longer exists adjacent to the Tunnel's southern entrance/exit. The pub on the right is the Princess Victoria, 9 Lower Road, which stood on the corner of Brunel Road. This is named after Marc Brunel who built the nearby Wapping-Rotherhithe tunnel, now part of the London Overground railway, assisted by his son, Isambard. On the left of the picture is the former Bermondsey Electricity Showroom. A large roundabout now covers this area in conjunction with road realignment and a grassed area. The first motor bus service to use Rotherhithe Tunnel was the 182 from 23 March 1927 and this service was renumbered 82 on 3 October 1934. The decline of London Docks caused the abandonment of the 82 but a new P4 service with narrow midibuses (due to tunnel width restrictions) was introduced in October 1988, succeeded by the 395. However, this was withdrawn on 29 April 2006 from which date no bus service has operated through the tunnel. (Edward Shepherd/London Bus Museum)

RT 4823 and a Bedford TK lorry stand at Gardiners Corner, Aldgate, ready to turn from Whitechapel High Street into Commercial Road in March 1969. On the extreme left an entrance to Aldgate East underground station is visible. Despite this area now being dominated by sky scrapers the three nearest buildings survive but Gardiners enormous six-storey department store with clock tower which overlooked the junction has been demolished after being gutted by fire in 1972. Bedford TK lorries were in general production from 1960-1986 (this one dates from 1965) and for military use until 1992. RT 4823 from Barking garage, numerically the third last RT, is carrying a Saunders roofbox body which it acquired in 1966 from RT 4220. The bus was withdrawn in April 1970 and sold. It is believed to still exist. This manifestation of route 23 (Becontree-Aldgate) was withdrawn in 18 May 1985 after its length was reduced from the 1970s and the surviving section was replaced by re-routeing the 15. (Edward Shepherd/London Bus Museum)

When this picture of RT 4263 was taken in Rochester Way, Eltham, just one week remained of Poplar garage operation of the 108A before the allocation was switched to New Cross garage on 26 October 1968. RTs had succeeded RTLs in the previous month but had to surrender weekend working to RMs on 22 March 1969 and the service, which had started on 19 April 1944, was withdrawn on 24 January 1970. RT 4263 was withdrawn in February 1973 and scrapped, which is probably the same fate which befell the 1964 Ford Zephyr 6 heading towards the photographer. The church in the background, St Barnabas on the corner of Cobbett Road, has had an interesting history. Designed by Sir George Gilbert Scott whose work includes St Pancras Station Hotel, this ecclesiastic building was originally erected in 1858 in Woolwich Dockyard. It was dismantled and rebuilt in Rochester Way with some alterations in 1932/1933 but in 1944 it was badly damaged by enemy action which included the destruction of its roof and interior. It was finally restored in 1956. (Edward Shepherd/ London Bus Museum)

Due to a low bridge in the Harrow area which RLH 27 has just passed under, and prior to the relaxation of regulations preventing long single deckers, the busy 230 service was operated by lowbridge double deckers from Harrow Weald garage, new RLHs replacing STLs from 6 May 1953. Occasionally, the garage would run short of red buses and borrow a green one from the Country Area. This occurred for the last time between July 1968 and the replacement of the 230 by the new OPO route HI on 15 June 1969 during which time RLH 27, seen here in May 1969, was borrowed. During its extensive loan period it acquired a Central Area radiator badge, as seen here. Because of its unique status at Harrow Weald this bus was chosen to operate the final service and, following its use on a subsequent farewell tour over the route, was withdrawn and exported to the USA in September 1969. In this view the vehicle is travelling along a section of Headstone Drive which is now blocked off to traffic. The building behind the bus is now occupied at street level by shops (1-13 Headstone Lane) and abuts Holy Trinity church. The building to the left has been completely remodelled. (Capital Transport)

The girls of Wilmington Grammar School seem to be more interested in the photographer than the buses in this 1969 view of Market Place, Dartford. Purpose-built bus stands have since been installed here but the buildings in the background are unchanged. The 477 is now operated by Arriva and still serves the same places today (Orpington, Swanley, Wilmington and Dartford etc) but has been extended to Bluewater. The buses are from Swanley garage: from left to right they are RT 3244 and RT 4745. Both were transferred to LCBS in 1970 but RT 3244 was repurchased by LT in September 1972 and painted red. It was sold for scrap in December 1974. RT 4745 suffered the same fate when withdrawn by LCBS in July 1971. (W Ryan)

Route 21A commenced operation in March 1941 running non-stop from Woolwich (Parsons Hill) to Eltham and then continuing to Sidcup, Swanley and Farningham. RTs were replaced by OPO Merlins on 26 October 1968 and this view depicts MB 308 twelve months later. Swifts took over on 24 November 1973 and following subsequent operation by DMSs and Titans the service was withdrawn on 27 October 1984 and replaced by new route 233. MB 308 entered service in October 1968 at Sidcup garage and remained there until November 1973. Following withdrawal in July 1975 the vehicle was exported to Australia and was still in service into the 1990s. This picture was taken from Church Road, Sidcup looking along the High Street. The Black Horse pub closed in 2008 and was demolished three years later to make way for a Travelodge. The developers were required to erect a fake facade of the pub in front of part of the Travelodge but their first attempt was considered unacceptable. Version 2 is regarded as an improvement. (Edward Shepherd/London Bus Museum)

Nine buses line up in Crystal Palace Parade in early 1970. Most are RMs but the second vehicle is an RF and there are some RTs near the back. A bus station has since been built just forward of the front bus, thereby eliminating the need for terminating buses to park in the road. Route 2 was cut back from its former extremities of Golders Green and Crystal Palace on 13 June 1970 and withdrawn entirely in 1997. The 227, which was converted from RFs to SMSs on 2 January 1971, still terminates at Crystal Palace but the 63 was truncated to Honor Oak in 2003. The front three buses are RM 1758, which visited Hamburg in September-October 1969, RF 396 and RM 1421. The latter was re-registered AEW 440A in 1990. The mast belongs to the radio and TV transmitting station which became operational in 1956 and is said to have been the tallest structure in London until 1 Canada Square at Canary Wharf was erected in 1991. (Lindsay Bridge)

Dalston garage's 178 service had the distinction of being the last RLH route operated by either LT or London Country. It was a late starter, originating on 13 May 1959 as a replacement for RF-operated route 208A. The requirement for a larger capacity vehicle could not be met by RTs and RMs because of a low bridge in Carpenter's Road but RLHs would just fit (subject to a 5mph speed limit!) and there happened to be spare red RLHs available following the withdrawal of Merton's 127 service some nine months earlier. In this view from March 1971 RLH 64 has just crossed the River Lea in White Post Lane just before this becomes Carpenter's Road. Surprisingly, despite the proximity of the Olympic Park, this location is easily recognisable today, with both large buildings still extant. Just over half of the RLH fleet of 76 vehicles survive, but not RLH 64. (David Christie)

The origins of route 236 can be traced back to 1926 when, as numbered 263 and suffixes, it ran between Finsbury Park and Hackney Wick and was operated by a variety of independent companies and ultimately by LGOC. LT renumbered the service 236 in 1934, putting it in the 2xx series for single deck routes because low bridges precluded the use of double deckers. This view of RFs 484 and 335 was taken in Rock Street, Finsbury Park, just before the RFs were replaced by OPO SMS buses on 17 April 1971, by which time the 236 had become the last crew-operated single deck route in London. The scene is instantly recognisable today, with the letter P having been straightened, but on the extreme left the telephone boxes have been removed. (Fred Ivey)

The East Ham and Barking By-pass (A13, Alfreds Way) is relatively quiet in this view from May 1971 but the road has since been widened to three lanes in each direction and has become a magnet for huge lorries. The widening has meant the loss of some of the front gardens of the houses on the extreme left, the removal of the square arches on the bridge over the River Roding and the repositioning of the footbridge used by the photographer. Victor Blagden & Co, which specialised in the manufacture of steel drums (a pile can be seen near the bridge), has vacated its site at Gascoigne Wharf on the left and a Bestway warehouse now occupies the site. Gascoigne Road is on the right. Upton Park's RT 929 is on its way to North Romford from Dagenham on a 175 working. DMS buses were already operating on Sundays when the RTs were replaced by ex-BEA Routemasters (RMAs) on 11 October 1975. After some eleven months RTs regained the route on Mondays-Saturdays due to the unsuitability of the RMAs on bus route work and standard RMs took over on 19 March 1977. Later that year RT 929 was withdrawn and sold for scrap. (Edward Shepherd/London Bus Museum)

RT 3066 climbs Upper Wickham Lane, East Wickham, in June 1971 against the distant backdrop of Plumstead Cemetery rising up behind Wickham Lane. The steeple visible to the right of the lamp post belongs to the cemetery chapel. The bus has just negotiated the roundabout where Wickham Lane changes to Upper Wickham Lane and is heading for Welling. The point at which this picture was taken is still largely rural today but the landscape is now obscured by trees. Under Stage 1 of the trolleybus replacement programme the 96 took over from the 696 (Dartford-Woolwich) on 4 March 1959. RTs were superseded by OPO DMS buses on 6 November 1971. RT 3066 arrived at Bexleyheath garage (the former trolleybus depot) in July 1969 from Aldenham Works and remained there until withdrawal in May 1972. It was then sold and converted into a mobile caravan. (Edward Shepherd/London Bus Museum).

In the heart of docklands two new DMS buses stand in Wapping High Street virtually opposite Wapping station on probably the first day of the conversion of route 67 from RM to OPO, 4 December 1971. This service remained DMS operated until Ms took over on 17 June 1982 by which time DMS 204 in the foreground had already been withdrawn. Replacing trolleybus route 647 on 19 July 1961, the 67 was noteworthy for being operated for a time by Leyland Atlanteans (XAs) and Country Area Daimler Fleetlines (XFs). Several prominent buildings in this area were huge warehouses, many of which survive through being converted into flats. This includes the Gun Wharf warehouse, the Wapping Lane frontage of which dominates the background of the picture. Even the small crane, part of which can be seen at the top of the building, remains attached to the wall today. (Fred Ivey)

The 78 (Dulwich to Shoreditch) replaced Tilling's long established horse bus service in 1913. RTs and RMs worked the 78 immediately prior to the route's conversion to OPO on 13 May 1972, when this photograph was taken. DMS 324, from the only batch with white relief, is descending Tower Bridge Approach heading northwards in this view taken when the bus was brand new. However, its shine was soon to fade for the vehicle was withdrawn seven years later, never to run again. On 24 February 1980 the DMS type was replaced on this route by the Scania MD class. Leyland National LS single deckers followed before they were quickly ousted by Titans in 1982. More dramatic change was to come to the 78 service in 1990 when green-livered London & Country vehicles took over. However, real drama had occurred on 30 December 1952 when RT 793 on a 78 service jumped a 3ft gap across the river because the bascules had started to rise without warning as the bus crossed Tower Bridge. The driver, Albert Gunter, was rewarded for his heroic action in saving his passengers because if the bus had remained on the rising bascule the consequences would have been catastrophic. (Fred Ivey)

Opposite: Three brand new DMS buses jostle for position in Malden Road among an array of road signs on the first day of the conversion of routes 213 and 213A from RT crew operation to OPO (5 August 1972). The location is Plough Green, Old Malden, which lies between Worcester Park and the A3 Kingston by-pass. This area, originally known as Malden, was renamed in 1870 as a result of the development of New Malden, some two miles away, beyond the A3. Today, the old wooden signpost and the fine chimney stack on the left have been removed, the wooden bus shelter has been replaced and the Plough public house, out of view on the right (a 15th century Grade II Listed building), has become a Steak House. The front two buses are brand new MCW-bodied DMSs 1276 and 1257 which were withdrawn in 1979 and sold by Ensigns to West Midlands PTE, lasting until 1983 and 1984 respectively before being scrapped. Route 213 (formerly LGOC route 113) was RF-operated until the road was lowered beneath Worcester Park railway bridge. That enabled RTs to take over from 8 May 1963, which was also the start date of the 213A service. (Fred Ivey)

Above: It is 12 August 1972, the first day of route 106's OPO conversion from RMs to DMS vehicles, and inspectors are on duty as passengers board DMS 1295 in Burdett Road, Limehouse. However, RMs made a come-back on 31 March 1979 only to be replaced by OPO Titans on 4 September 1982. This was the first day of service for Hackney garage's DMS 1295 and the bus clocked up just under seven years of London service before being sold to West Midland PTE in August 1979. This operator withdrew the vehicle in November 1983 and it was scrapped soon after. This location has changed considerably since 1972 although the modern building by the bus stop and the white one next to it on the corner of Commercial Road survive. The Londoner pub in the background, sandwiched between East India Dock Road (A13) and West India Dock Road, has been demolished for road widening. It was built in 1860 and originally called the Eastern Hotel. (Edward Shepherd/London Bus Museum)

Queen Anne, surrounded by four attendants, surveys Ludgate Hill and the railway bridge taking trains from Blackfriars to Holborn Viaduct. Its subsequent removal has improved the view of St Paul's Cathedral from Ludgate Circus. Queen Anne was the reigning monarch when the present St Paul's was completed in 1710. The current statue (Grade II Listed) was unveiled in 1886, replacing its damaged predecessor dating from 1710 which was saved by chance and is currently at Holmhurst St Mary, near Hastings with Grade II* Listing. RT 2639, photographed from the steps of St Paul's in August 1972, is operating route 15 to Upton Park (Boleyn). The bus was based at Upton Park garage from April 1963 to November 1972 and sent for scrap in July 1976. Route 15 originated in November 1908, operating between Shepherd's Bush and East Ham. (Edward Shepherd/London Bus Museum)

Against a background that is totally unrecognisable today, Poplar's RT 2652 heads for Cubitt Town from Smithfield, travelling along Westferry Road around September 1972. Route 277 was a bus replacement service for the 677 trolleybus introduced on 15 April 1959. RT 2652 was withdrawn in May 1975 and scrapped. The elevated sign on the brick wall to the left of the bus points to Ocean Wharf. This turning is now the entrance to an apartment block of that name overlooking the River Thames. On the left is St John McDougall Gardens, which also borders the river. (Edward Shepherd/London Bus Museum)

Camberwell's smart-looking RT 2998 had only one year of further service remaining prior to scrapping when this picture was taken in Norwood Road, Tulse Hill, during August 1972. The 172 from Forest Hill to Highgate was a replacement for tram route 35 and started on 7 April 1952 with RTs. These continued to operate the service, along with RTLs for a time, until 3 August 1975 when DMs took over. These were ousted by RMs on 3 June 1982 but their reign was short-lived because the route was withdrawn on 3 August 1985. The Tulse Hill Tavern, now called the Tulse Hill Hotel, stands on the corner of Norwood Road and the road called Tulse Hill. This prominent landmark was built in 1840 and its external appearance, acceptable in 1972, has been further enhanced in recent years. (R C Riley/Online Transport Archive)

In an attempt to provide buses in localities which were sometimes out of reach, for example in up-market areas where the residents would not appreciate what they regarded as a noisy, lumbering giant, LT started an experiment in 1972 running mini buses. The first batch of such vehicles consisted of twenty Strachans-bodied Ford Transits which were introduced on two new flat-fare services in September 1972, when this photograph was taken. This depicts FS 5 close to Brixton underground station operating the P4 (Brixton-Dulwich Village-Brockley Rise). However, such small vehicles quickly wore out and were replaced on the P4 by short Bristol LHs (BS class) on 18 December 1976. Residents were presumably becoming accustomed to larger vehicles because Leyland Nationals were allocated to the P4 from 29 January 1983. Meanwhile, FS 5 had been withdrawn in September 1979 and sold. This location is easily recognisable today, with Boots the Chemists still occupying these premises at 449 Brixton Road, on the corner of Electric Avenue. (Roy Marshall/ The Bus Archive)

This view dates from October 1972 and despite the passage of time some things never change. This is exemplified by the St Albans Road frontage of The White Hart where even the lettering is unaltered today, perhaps due to its Grade II Listing. However, Green Shield Stamps have certainly had their day. This promotion scheme was launched in 1958 but changes in consumer habits caused it to be rebranded Argos in 1973 as it had become more catalogue orientated. Meanwhile Winters garage and filling station on the right has become a carwash business. The bus stop island remains but with a modern bus shelter. Route 299 (Southgate station to Borehamwood) was a new service which started on 24 January 1970 with Potters Bar-based RTs. These were replaced by OPO buses such as SMS 683 on 3 July 1971. Indeed SMS 683 spent its entire LT life at Potters Bar from July 1971 until withdrawal in May 1978. However, it avoided immediate scrapping by being sold and eventually working for another operator. Route 299 was replaced by the 298 on 26 September 1980. (Capital Transport)

MB 388 finds itself on a building site as it threads its way through the Grahame Park housing estate in Colindale during December 1972. Along with the RAF Museum and the Hendon Police College the estate was built on the former Hendon Aerodrome which was developed by Claude Grahame –White in 1911, who also set up a flying school and aircraft factory there. Flying ceased in 1968 and residential development began. Route 79 to Northolt (Target) was extended from Colindale to Quakers Course, on the Estate, from 14 December 1972, Alperton-based MBs having replaced RTs on 25 October 1969. The route number originated in October 1934 when double deckers were introduced on the previous 219, resulting in the removal of the service from the single deck 2xx series. MB 388 was a single-door MCW-bodied AEC Merlin which entered service in February 1969 and eked out a typically short Merlin existence, being withdrawn in September 1975 and scrapped. Route 79 was withdrawn on 29 September 1984. The Grahame Park Estate is currently undergoing a major regeneration initiative which has created some controversy. (Capital Transport)

Taking a break from its normal duties on the 80A (Morden-Walton-on-the-Hill), Sutton-based RF 485 appears to be working an Epsom Downs race day special on 21 April 1973. It has just made its way from Belmont station to the Banstead cross roads on the A217 and has turned into Fir Tree Road as it heads for the Grandstand. The bus has just returned from overhaul at Aldenham and was allocated to Sutton garage from April 1973 until October 1976. Withdrawn in January 1978 RF 485 was sold but was scrapped a little later after being vandalised. When this picture was taken the bus stop seen here would normally have been served by RT-operated route 164 (Morden station-Belmont station-Epsom Town Centre). Today the stop is used by the 166 service from West Croydon to Epsom Hospital. (Edward Shepherd/London Bus Museum)

Summer flowers still bloom in the flower bed today at this largely unchanged part of Mill Hill Broadway. RF 499 has just negotiated Mill Hill Circus (in the background) on its journey from Arnos Grove tube station in May 1973 and is just about to pass the junction with the appropriately named Flower Lane. The 251 was a renumbering in 1934 of route 551 which was started in 1925 by Redburn's Motor Services and ran between Whetstone and Edmonton (where there was a low bridge) via Arnos Grove. The service quickly attracted other independents, as well as the LGOC. RFs were introduced on to the 251 on 6 May 1953, sharing the service with TDs, and then took over completely on 1 May 1957. They remained in charge until superseded by BLs on 3 January 1977. Some two months earlier RF499, which had operated from Edgware garage since July 1965, was withdrawn and sold to a scrap merchant. (Capital Transport)

The 1970s marked the first period in LT's history when several Central Area buses operated in a livery other than red. The trend for carrying all-over advertising started in August 1969 and RML 2701, seen here in Haymarket during September 1972, carried tartan livery promoting Youngers Breweries from May 1972 until August 1973. In this picture the bus is operating from Holloway garage for a period of some three months. It was withdrawn in March 2004 and is now available for wedding hire based in Wigan carrying normal red London livery. The distinctive building with pedimented portico and six Corinthian columns is the Grade I Listed Theatre Royal Haymarket designed by John Nash which opened on this site in 1821. In September 1972 the theatre was staging the play entitled A Voyage Round My Father. (Roy Marshall/ The Bus Archive).

RT 2047, working route 133 from Liverpool Street, progresses gingerly along King William Street as it approaches the new London Bridge which opened in March 1973, some three months before this picture was taken. The Brixton-based RT is descending the 'umbrella' covering Upper and Lower Thames Street (one leads into the other at this point) which was being widened into a dual carriageway, requiring a longer overbridge. A few of the buildings still survive including the former House of Fraser building in the distance. From 1890 to 1900 King William Street had the City & South London Railway terminus at the junction with Monument Street (on the right) but the line was subsequently rerouted away from this station because of interchange difficulties. RTs were replaced on the 133 on 23 March 1975 and RT 2047 was consigned to the scrapyard in 1978. (Edward Shepherd/ London Bus Museum)

Continuing the theme of buses carrying all-over advertising, RM 1740 carried the livery of Danone from March–November 1973. From 1983 to 1991 it was employed as a Training vehicle, which included use as a Chiswick skid bus, and was then exported to Uruguay. The vehicle is seen passing the Wellington Arch at Hyde Park Corner. The Arch was completed in 1827 and was originally intended to be an outer entrance to Buckingham Palace. Instead, it became the so-called entrance to London, adjacent to Apsley House, the Duke of Wellington's residence, which was known informally as No 1, London. In the early 1880s the arch was repositioned to make way for road improvements and as a result of further traffic changes in 1962 it is now in the middle of the Hyde Park Corner roundabout. (Geoff Morant)

This scene at Elephant & Castle, Southwark, dating from May 1973 is dominated by the huge office block, Hannibal House, which was completed in 1965 and is built above the large Shopping Centre behind the bus. This part of London was badly bombed during the Second World War and was regenerated in the 1960s but it now due to be rebuilt again. Elephant & Castle, which is believed to have been named after a coaching inn of that name which no longer exists, has been a major cross roads since Roman times and RM 1781 is seen here negotiating the gyratory system. The Tottenham-based bus is working a 171 service which was introduced on 7 April 1952 to replace the 33 tram route. RMs took over from RTs and RTLs on 7 September 1968 and were superseded on 16 September 1986 by Leyland Titans which had already taken over Sunday workings in the previous year. RM 1781 was withdrawn in August 1982 and scrapped. (Capital Transport)

This scene at Southwark Bridge after 28 May 1973 (Spring Bank Holiday) depicts two bus routes on diversion, the 44 and the 133, both of which would normally use London Bridge. Route 44 (London Bridge Station-Mitcham and later to Aldgate for some journeys on Sundays and Bank Holidays to serve Petticoat Lane market) became operational on 1 October 1950 as a replacement for tram service 12. OPO DMS buses replaced RTs on 17 June 1972 which is when the example seen here, Wandsworth's DMS 384, entered service. It was withdrawn in July 1982 and subsequently sold for scrap. The bus behind is RT 2732 from Brixton garage working a 133 service from Liverpool Street to Streatham garage. This bus was withdrawn in May 1977 and exported to Switzerland. RTs were replaced on the 133 by crewed DMs on 23 March 1975. Southwark Bridge was opened in 1921 and the only alterations from the angle of this picture are replacement lamps of more traditional appearance and the removal of the police telephone on the extreme left. The bollard in the foreground is still in situ at the top of the flight of steps. However, the building backdrop has changed. (Edward Shepherd/London Bus Museum)

At first glance this Routemaster (RM 468) from North Street (Romford) garage seems to have lost its way in early 1975 but it is actually about to turn round at the Cripsey Avenue terminus of the 175A in Chipping Ongar. Taking over a section of the 175, this route only operated from 16 June 1973 until 8 January 1977 when it was replaced by the 247B. The service only required the use of one bus daily (an RT or RM) making just five journeys down Moreton Road (where it is seen here) to the junction with Cripsey Avenue. From 2 December 1974 two further journeys were added but these were diverted away from Cripsey Avenue to serve Ongar Comprehensive School. Moreton Road continued beyond the location seen here, crossing the bridge over Cripsey Brook in the centre of the picture and onwards to Moreton. RM 468 entered service in 1960 and was withdrawn in 1986, whereupon it was scrapped. (Geoff Morant)

RM 1055 from New Cross garage is surrounded by history as it crosses Blackfriars Bridge in June 1975. The road bridge was opened in 1869, replacing an earlier structure, and on the right is the former London, Chatham & Dover Railway (LC&DR) bridge built in 1864 serving St Paul's station, later renamed Blackfriars. This girder bridge was replaced by a new railway bridge built alongside and the old one was removed in 1985 leaving the support pillars although some have been incorporated into the widened railway bridge which now carries lengthened platforms over the river. Behind the bus is Bridge House (181 Queen Victoria Street) built in 1889 which is casting a shadow over the LC&DR iron coat of arms. These have since been removed although the ones on the southern abutment across the river survive. Route 141 was a replacement for the 641 trolleybus service and started on 8 November 1961 running between Grove Park and Winchmore Hill (curtailed to Wood Green from 7 September 1968). RM 1055 was withdrawn in August 1992 and scrapped. (Capital Transport)

With The Spotted Dog pub occupying the gabled building in the background and the Barking Dog on the ground floor of the office block behind, this town should need no introduction! Descending Longbridge Road from Barking railway station in June 1975 is RT 4027, a resident of Barking garage from October 1972 until withdrawal in July 1977 and subsequent export to France. Route 87, which operated between Rainham and Harold Hill at this time, saw its RTs replaced by RMs on 28 October 1978 except for a single Saturday working. This remained the case until the last day of RT operation in passenger service took place amid great ceremonial commiserations on 7 April 1979 with the conversion of Barking's route 62 to RMs during the day. This date marked the end of forty years of public service by the RT type, at least in London. A few still operate today in California! (Capital Transport)

RT 579 arrives at Heathrow Airport Central to terminate there in July 1975 and its blinds have already been set for its shortened eastern destination of East Acton (Ducane Road) rather than Shepherds Bush. Route 105 was shared between Southall and Shepherds Bush garages until 31 January 1981 and this RT is Southall-based. The state of the roof suggests that it is overdue for a repaint and unusually it is carrying a cream – coloured fleetname instead of the normal gold lettering. The bus was withdrawn in April 1978 and scrapped. Route 105 was extended from Southall to Heathrow on 6 January 1973 and continued to be served by RTs until RMs took over on 30 April 1978. In the background is Terminal 1, a state of the art passenger building when it opened in 1968 but which was closed in 2015 and is expected to be demolished to improve runway access for the current generation of huge aircraft. (Michael Harries/Author's collection)

The 290 was introduced on 7 September 1968 as a replacement for the 90C service and was initially an OPO RF route. BLs took over on 9 May 1976 and this picture was taken on the next day. BLs were in turn replaced by M double deckers on 4 September 1982. The location is the route's Hammersmith terminus outside the Metropolitan Line Underground station (redesignated as the Hammersmith & City Line station since 1990). The brick station building was designed by the Great Western Railway's architect, P E Culverhouse, and completed in 1909. At one time the original Hammersmith & City Railway was jointly owned by the Metropolitan Railway and the GWR. Various car owners have disregarded the No Parking signs but the two female traffic wardens seem to be ignoring the cars, presumably because this lay-by is on private land. The odd-looking all-red Underground logo was an idea of the time that did not last long. (Fred Ivey)

This bird's eye view of Rectory Road, Beckenham, in May 1976 finds DMS 1266 on its way to Bexleyheath garage on a 126 service. The bus has just left Beckenham Junction station which is out of view on the right, behind Twiggs Motors. A shoe repair business now occupies this corner section of the property. Route 126 (Beckenham Junction station-Bromley North station- Eltham) commenced on 1 September 1940 when double deckers were introduced on the 254, renumbering being necessary at that time because 2xx route numbers were confined to single deck routes. DMS buses operated the 126 only for a relatively short period, from 27 April 1975 until replaced by Leyland Nationals on 21 October 1979. A couple of months earlier DMS 1266 had been sold for scrap when just seven years old. (R C Riley/Online Transport Archive)

In the second half of the 1970s Birmingham and Midland Motor Omnibus Company (BMMO) open-top D9 double deckers were a familiar sight working LT's Round London Sightseeing Tour. Prince Marshall's Obsolete Fleet Company purchased ten ex-Midland Red D9s between 1974 and 1980, converting the first seven into open-toppers, and hiring them all to LT. The particular vehicle seen here at Westminster Bridge, turning out of Embankment and heading for Parliament Square in July 1976, entered service with Midland Red at Stafford in January 1963. Numbered 5035, it was withdrawn in November 1974 and then passed to Obsolete Fleet, becoming OM 6. It has since been preserved. In the background is County Hall, the former headquarters of the defunct Greater London Council. This building was completed in 1922 and now houses various tourist attractions as well as providing hotel accommodation. The London Eye would now dominate the background behind the bus. (Mike Russell)

This view of Clarence Street, Kingston, dates from 19 July 1976, the second day of BL operation on route 264 following the replacement of RFs. This route from Kingston to Hersham had started on 3 May 1950 but only lasted until 27 January 1978 as a result of local government subsidy cuts. Single deckers were required because of a low bridge at Hersham station. BL 30 entered service for the RF/BL conversion and was withdrawn in January 1983, after which it was exported to Guernsey. DMS 608 on the right had an equally short LT life, entering service in May 1973 and being exported to Hong Kong in 1980. Behind the DMS the rear of an RF can be seen entering Eden Street on a 215, 218 or 219 service. This section of Clarence Street has since been pedestrianised and most of the buildings remain. The Littlewoods store is now occupied by Marks & Spencer. (Fred Ivey)

There is still a letter R fixed to the modern bus stop that stands outside No 48 Camden Road, Camden Town, but much has changed at this location since this photograph was taken in October 1976. The Aerated Bread Company (ABC) bakery on the left ceased production in 1982 and has been replaced by a Sainsbury's supermarket which is Grade II listed due to its apparent futuristic architecture. The bus is Park Royal-bodied Leyland B15 prototype No 4 which entered service in May 1976 and was returned to Leyland in April 1978. It was later re-registered UJI 6314. This class of bus came to be called the Titan and, following the success of the trial, LT ordered 1125 new vehicles of this type. Whereas the prototype Routemasters were labelled London's Bus of the Future this was changed on the B15, as evidenced here, to London's Bus of Tomorrow. (Capital Transport)

Overleaf: It is Christmas time in Cranbrook Road, Ilford, probably in December 1976. The 148 (Dagenham-Leytonstone) was worked from Seven Kings garage where RT 4190 was based from September 1975 (following a repaint at Aldenham) until October 1977. The route was converted to OPO DMSs on 23 July 1977 and withdrawn on 20 March 1993. RT 4190 continued work as a trainer and was withdrawn in August 1979. It escaped being scrapped, unlike most of its contemporaries, and has been preserved. In this picture, the bus is passing Rigby Mews. This scene has not altered over the years apart from the creation of a high rise development in the distance and the normal changes in retail ownership. For example, the building on the left is no longer a Tesco branch. (Melvyn Morgan/Author's collection)

LT made a great effort to celebrate HM The Queen's Silver Jubilee in 1977 by painting twenty-five RMs in silver livery and temporarily renumbering them SRM 1-25. The costs were partly defrayed by the sponsorship of individual buses which carried the sponsors' advertising. The vehicle seen here is RM 1904, temporarily renumbered SRM 19, and was sponsored by Nescafe. It received its silver livery in February 1977 and was based at Streatham garage. In January 1985 it was withdrawn from service and exported to Canada in the following year. In this view from July 1977 SRM 19 is proceeding along Baker Street on its journey from West Hampstead to Thornton Heath. RMs had replaced RTs on the 159 on 3 August 1975 and this service was the last to be operated by Routemasters, conversion to OPO taking place on 10 December 2005. Thus ended crew operation in London, apart from the two heritage routes (now down to one). This part of Baker Street is largely unchanged today. The large building in the background on the left is the Metropolitan Railway's Chiltern Court apartment block above Baker Street station in Marylebone Road, completed in 1929. (Capital Transport)

The passengers on this No 27 bus in July 1977 probably think they are riding on a new type of Routemaster but in fact they are travelling in a 1959 ex-Leeds Corporation vehicle. This Roe-bodied Daimler CVG6 was a test bed for experimental Dennis-Voith engineering to be used in a future new type, the Dennis Dominator, and was doing the rounds of various operators, albeit in LT red livery (but with no fleet name). LT was not overenthusiastic about the Dominator and only bought three (HI-3) but several were in use in London with other operators (eg for sightseeing). In this photograph the bus is heading along Beadon Road, Hammersmith and has just turned off Glenthorne Road. The Dartmouth Castle pub is still standing, attached to an office block (Glen House). The houses behind the bus have been replaced by a similar style of building, the Luma Concept Hotel. (Alan Murray)

A chance meeting of two RFs passing in Lammas Lane, Esher, in July 1977 presented a unique photographic opportunity for the cameraman. Heading up the hill is a very lucky vehicle, RF 489, which after withdrawal in November 1977 was snapped up by Queen Eleanor School in Guildford and then acquired for preservation in August 1982. Hopefully, the smoking exhaust has now been rectified! Coming down the hill towards the roundabout serving West End Lane is RF 533 which was withdrawn in October 1977 and bought by Continental Pioneer of Richmond for spares, before being scrapped. Route 218 (Kingston-Staines) started life as the 62 in 1922 and was renumbered in 1934. It currently runs as a 458. Low bridges prevent the use of double deckers so Swifts were meant to have replaced the RFs on both the 218 and 219 in 1977 but were too large to fit over the pits at Kingston garage. Twenty-five RFs (but not these two) were rehabilitated and used until 1979 when the routes were moved to operate from Norbiton where the replacement LNs could fit over the pits. (Alan Murray)

In the north west reaches of the London Borough of Hillingdon lies the village of Harefield and on 3 September 1977 (the date of this picture) Council-sponsored route 128 commenced operation using new BL buses from Uxbridge garage. These were the last of the class (BL 93-5) and were painted in a special red and yellow livery. The service ran daily between Ruislip Station and Harefield Hospital via Mount Vernon Hospital with some journeys to Rickmansworth station and four to the rural location shown here, Harefield West via Park Lane (not the London one!). LSs took over from the BLs on 13 July 1988 and the route was withdrawn on 17 August 1991, replaced by new route R1 and adjustments to the U1. Meanwhile, BL 93 was withdrawn in August 1988 and sold. Today, the U9 uses this stand in Park Lane located at the junction with Shelley Lane although the bus stop is marked Belfry Avenue which is further away. This scene is unchanged apart from the wooden fence having been replaced by a low brick wall. (Alan Murray)

RT 2695 pounds along the dual carriageway of the North Circular Road in Oakthorpe Park, Palmers Green, on route 34 from Barnet on one of its last journeys before the service was converted to OPO with DMS buses on 10 September 1977. In the following month the bus was withdrawn and sold for scrap. The 34 currently runs from Barnet to Walthamstow but even with the cutting back from Leytonstone it is still one of the longest bus routes in London. This suburban scene from 1977 has changed over the years as road traffic has increased. Although some nearby parts of the North Circular Road have pleasant central reservations with some greenery this section now has a very urban appearance with crash barriers installed and virtually every house has had its front garden concreted over for off-road car parking. (Capital Transport)

People are piling aboard RT 1688 as it picks up in The Broadway, Greenford, near the junction with Oldfield Lane (marked by the trees), before heading northwards in September 1977. RTs lasted on Southall garage's route 120 until 28 January 1978 when OPO was introduced using DMS vehicles although these had already taken over the Sunday services in the previous October. RT 1688 had a short existence at Southall, having moved from Sidcup earlier in 1977 and being withdrawn at Southall in March 1978, followed by scrapping. In front of the RT is a Swift on route 273, a new service running from Ealing Broadway to Ruislip introduced on 30 November 1968 using RTs until 6 January 1973. The route was withdrawn on 2 June 1984. (Capital Transport)

It is hard to believe that one could travel around central London between 1972 and 1983 in a 1930 open staircase ST bus. During this period LT operated Vintage Bus Service 100 with vehicles provided by Obsolete Fleet, normally ST 922. This former Thomas Tilling AEC Regent I dating from 1930 was absorbed into LT on the latter's creation in 1933, one of 191 such vehicles. ST 922 was withdrawn in 1939 and quickly reinstated because of the Second World War. Hired for a time to Midland General it returned to service in London in late 1944 and was withdrawn again in December 1946. Instead of being scrapped the bus was converted into a staff canteen (693J) and then sold in 1955 to British Road Services. It was subsequently found in a scrapyard and purchased for preservation in December 1966. ST 922 is now part of the London Bus Museum collection at Brooklands and in 2016 was returned to Tilling livery with fleet number 6098. This picture was taken in September 1977 in Victoria as the bus pulled out of Vauxhall Bridge Road. It is "off-route" and carrying no passengers so the crew may be taking a lunch break. (Alan Murray)

These buses seem to be huddled together in the cold as they stand in the former LGOC Kingston Bus Station. This opened in 1928, six years after the garage to which it was attached, and was a familiar landmark in Clarence Street, close to the railway station, until its closure on 17 May 2000 and subsequent demolition. The Rotunda complex now stands in its place but the Granada cinema building on the right still exists and has been turned into a nightclub. This picture from February 1978 depicts, from left to right, RF 512, RF 381 (both preserved), BL 40, an unidentified RF and BL, RM 2010 (later exported to the USA), RM 2026 (hidden) and RT 3951. RTs worked route 71 (Mon-Sats) until RMs took over on 4 March 1978. The RFs remained on the 218 and 219 until their last day on 30 March 1979. (Roy Hobbs/Online Transport Archive)

The centre of Blackheath is hilly, as evidenced by this panoramic view featuring RM 945 climbing up Lee Road in early April 1978 working Route 54 (Croydon-Woolwich). With the opening of TramLink the 54 was cut back from Croydon to Elmers End on 10 June 2000. On 22 April 1978 the RTs and RMs which shared the 54 were replaced by OPO DMS vehicles. The RM in the distance is on a 192 service to Lewisham. This was another RT/RM shared service until RMs took over entirely on 4 May 1976 and the route also became OPO DMS on 22 April 1978. The reign of RMs on these two routes would in fact end some two weeks after the date of this picture. All the buildings in this picture are still standing but the Armed Forces careers information offices on the extreme right are no longer there. This photograph is rather misleading in terms of the road layout because, at the foot of the hill, the road rather confusingly called Blackheath Village, curves sharply to the left. From this viewpoint the large building on the left of the picture is actually on the right hand side of the main road! (Chris Evans)

RM 1428 heads for Ilford Broadway on Route 86 (Romford-Limehouse) on a short service to Bow Church in September 1978. This view is in High Road, Ilford, as the bus passes Elizabeth Avenue on the left and Ilford (Buckingham Road) Cemetery behind the railings on the right. The car showroom has since shut down and the end section of that building together with the one behind the bus have been replaced. This iteration of Route 86 was introduced on 19 August 1959 but its history is complicated because it tended to be intertwined with the 86A over the years. Under the Bassom scheme of route numbering in 1924, the 86 was created but it was previously LGOC's service 26 (Stratford – Brentwood). RM 1428 was withdrawn in February 1994. (Capital Transport)

Leslie Whyte founded Whyte's Airport Services in the 1960s primarily to transfer airline passengers around Heathrow Airport. The company built up a fleet of coaches including 35 Ford R1014s, most of which were fitted with extra-wide nearside and offside doors providing easy access for passengers with luggage and were not licensed to run on public roads as they operated airside and on internal roads. The company also obtained a contract with BR Southern Region to provide the Heathrow end of a rail/air coach link for passengers travelling from Waterloo to Feltham. Three licensed traditional coaches were available for this service, an example of which is this Willowbrook-bodied Ford R1014, No 27 (RPP 134M) making its way along Bedfont Lane to Feltham station. The vehicle was delivered new to Whyte's in May 1974 and is seen here in March 1979 passing the junction with Southville Road. Whyte's merged with Capital Coaches to form Capital Logistics in April 1997, which in turn was sold to Tellings-Golden Miller in April 2000. (Alan Murray)

George Shillibeer inaugurated the first bus service in London, from Paddington to Bank, in 1829 and to commemorate the 150th anniversary of this event several London buses were painted in "Shillibeer livery" in 1979. One such vehicle was RM 2158, seen here in early 1979 in Oxford Street, which is about to terminate at Oxford Circus with its next destination already shown as Stoke Newington, its long time northern terminus. Route 73 was introduced on 30 November 1914 running between Kings Cross and Barnes and for much of its existence its south western terminus was Richmond or Kingston. It was converted to OPO on 4 September 2004. RM 2158 was one of forty RMs sent to Sri Lanka in 1988 following withdrawal and is still at work. Not surprisingly, its present external appearance is a far cry from the resplendent state seen here as it enters Oxford Circus. Most of the buildings in this view are still extant and Top Shop remains in occupation. The delivery van is turning into Regent Street. It belongs to the Evening News which ceased publication in 1980 (apart from a very short renaissance in 1987) following its merger with the Evening Standard. (Capital Transport)

In June 1979 King's College School in Wimbledon celebrated its 150th Anniversary which also coincided with LT's Shillibeer 150th Anniversary celebrations. In this view school children and staff are riding on a c.1890 Four Light Garden Seat horse bus. "Four Light" refers to having four windows on each side. "Garden Seat" means that the upper deck seats face forward, conforming to today's buses, instead of having the earlier "knifeboard" configuration with central longitudinal bench and passengers seated back to back. The bus was first operated by the Andrews Star Omnibus Company and was repurchased by the family in 1988 who have since donated it to the London Bus Museum at Brooklands. When seen here the bus was carrying wording denoting Kings Cross, Victoria and Piccadilly Circus. It is travelling along Ridgway, Wimbledon, with Clifton Road on the left behind the tree and the Swan public house in the distance. All the houses remain in situ. (Alan Murray)

LT's Shop Linker service was a bold initiative in 1979 to provide a regular shuttle service between London's major stores in the West End, Kensington and Knightsbridge using sixteen standard RMs painted in a striking red and yellow livery. The buses were intended to be sponsored by retailers who would provide music and advertising over a p/a system but several remained unsponsored including RM 2167, photographed here travelling south along Regent Street in April 1979. The service started on 7 April 1979, coinciding with the last day of RTs operating in normal public service, and ended on 28 September 1979, never to be repeated. A flat fare of 30p was charged but the fare was quickly removed from the front blind display because of complaints, presumably from short-sighted people, that this gave the impression of a bus running on route 30, which ironically ran over some of the Shop Linker route. The flat fare was in fact more than the normal bus fare and much of the route was already covered by cheaper and more reliable or direct traditional bus services. Consequently, Shop Linker was not the outstanding success that had been anticipated. RM 2167 reverted to all-red livery in October 1979 and was withdrawn in June 1987, followed by scrapping. (Capital Transport)

One of LT's more rural routes was the 146 from Bromley North to Downe. This was RT-operated until 22 April 1978 when OPO BLs took over. However, RMs had taken over Sunday workings from 26 January 1975 despite the narrow lanes which made RT-operation more practicable. This view from early November 1979 when the trees were still in leaf depicts BL 80 from Bromley garage. This bus remained in service until April 1993 before being sold. Here, it is operating a short journey to The Fox at Keston. This pub is located in Heathfield Road immediately behind the photographer. The pub sign behind the bus relates to the Greyhound in Commonside. There is now a mini roundabout at this junction but otherwise little has changed. In the distance to the right of the road sign is a stone drinking fountain which was erected in Bromley Market in the 1870s and was moved to its present site in 1937. (R C Riley/Online Transport Archive)

Following approval of the prototype Routemaster coach, CRL 4 (later designated RMC 4), LT decided to order 68 similar vehicles for the busier Green Line coach routes to supplement the RF fleet. When LCBS decided to dispense with its RMCs in the late 1970s, having demoted them to bus work, LT acquired them to use as trainers. RMC 1480 is seen on such duties in Haymarket in May 1980 with LT markings applied to its Leaf Green livery but still carrying worn out advertisements promoting Golden Rovers and encouraging potential drivers to apply to any LCBS garage. After being re-registered KGJ 52A RMC 1480 was withdrawn in April 1992 and sold abroad. Behind the coach is Upton Park's RML 2523. Today, the buildings seen here in Haymarket are still extant but with the advertising removed. Behind the last two buses is Coventry Street named after Henry Coventry, Secretary of State to King Charles II. The gabled building remains in place but the other two have been redeveloped. (Author)

LT's misfortunes arising from unsuitable new bus types from the late 1960s into the 1980s might have been avoided if the front entrance, rear-engined Routemaster had entered production. However FRM I, seen here in Pall Mall in May 1980, was a one-off prototype. Developed by AEC and Park Royal, 80% of the vehicle comprised parts from standard RMs. FRM I entered service in June 1967 and, after working on a few different routes, was allocated to the Round London Sightseeing Tour in January 1978. On its withdrawal from this duty in February 1983 it was presented to the London Transport Museum. Alongside FRM I is a Metro-Scania Metropolitan (MD class) on a 53 service from Plumstead to Camden Town. This version of Route 53 originated in 1913, operating between Maida Vale and Plumstead. Pall Mall derives its name from a 17th century ball game similar to croquet. All the buildings are still standing and the one nearest the camera on the left has been much improved through exterior cleaning. The National Gallery in Trafalgar Square is visible in the distance. (Author)

Titan T 9 heads for Rainham War Memorial in this view dating from 10 May 1980. The bus had entered service at Hornchurch garage on March 1979 and was sold to Blue Triangle in 2001. The 165, starting at Collier Row, was introduced in 1940 as a double deck replacement for the single deck 253. This latter route originated in 1934, in effect replacing an Imperial Omnibus service between Romford and Rainham introduced in 1927. The 165, subsequently extended to Havering Park, was crew-operated with RMLs at the time of conversion to OPO DMSs on 16 June 1973. These were replaced by Titans on 4 December 1978. The location of this picture is Rosewood Avenue, Hornchurch, at the junction with Aldingham Gardens and no great change has occurred over some forty years apart from a house extension and the loss of a couple of chimney stacks. (Alan Mortimer)

Photographed at Holborn Circus in May 1980, Chalk Farm's DMS 6 entered service in December 1971 and clocked up some eleven years of LT service before ending up as a mobile cafe in France. RM-operated route 46 was introduced on 8 January 1972 replacing part of the 45, with OPO DMS buses taking over some five months later. These remained on this service until 30 August 1984 when Ms took over. Today the route has been extended to run between Lancaster Gate and Bart's Hospital but still goes via Hampstead meaning that it is far quicker to travel by Underground between the terminal points than to take the 46 bus! The striking statue dates from 1874 and shows Prince Albert and his horse in an unusually jaunty pose. It has since been moved slightly westwards due to road improvements. (R C Riley/Online Transport Archive)

There are problems at Penge on 18 June 1980 because LS 346 is suffering from a flat battery and requires a jump start from another Leyland National while LS 328 watches from a distance. The location is the Crooked Billet terminus, the pub being situated behind the rescue bus. The Tudor revival buildings in the background are the former Watermen and Lightermen's alms houses (c. 1840), now privately owned, consisting of side blocks surrounding a courtyard (Watermen's Square). The 227 service dates back to 1916 when it was LGOC route 109 and was introduced to bring munitions personnel to Woolwich Arsenal from a wider catchment area during the First World War. With the subsequent agreement of the LGOC the service was operated from Tilling's Bromley garage (coded TB) from 1924, where these Leyland Nationals were based. The 109 was renumbered 227 in 1934 following LT's creation and both routes were always operated by single deckers due to the low bridge at Shortlands. (R C Riley/Online Transport Archive)

The Free Ferry terminus of route 69 at North Woolwich (Pier Road) seems quite busy in this August 1980 view as RM 422 in the foreground waits to return to Chingford Mount. The 69 was introduced on 3 February 1960, replacing trolleybus route 669, but no longer serves North Woolwich. The rotunda building is the northside entrance to the Woolwich pedestrian tunnel under the River Thames which is Grade II listed, along with the southern rotunda. Both date from 1912 when the tunnel opened. The building in the background on the right has been demolished but the one behind RM 422 is still extant. It is the former North Woolwich railway station built in 1854 for the North London Railway. The station was closed in 2006 and the Great Eastern Railway Museum which occupied the building and the associated trackside area is no longer in occupation. (Mike Russell)

RM 411 crosses Connaught Road and the Palace Gates – North Woolwich railway line using the Silvertown Bypass in August 1980. Silvertown was so named after an entrepreneur, Stephen Silver, who set up various factories in the area from 1852. The bypass, which was little more than a quarter of a mile long, was opened in 1935 primarily to alleviate traffic congestion at a level crossing beside Silvertown station, given the volume of road vehicles travelling to and from the three Royal Docks. It formed part of a 1930s major road building project in the area and supplemented the elevated Silvertown Way. The docks ceased to operate in 1981 when cargo handling was transferred to Tilbury and the bypass was closed to traffic in 1991. RM 411 is passing over the bow string girder bridge which was demolished in 1995. This iconic structure was made of reinforced concrete and had a 109 foot span. (Mike Russell)

Upton Park's RML 2494 visits Cyprus, a developing area of Beckton that followed the opening of the Royal Docks. The locality was named after the Mediterranean island after Britain took control of the territory in 1878. The bus is travelling along Cyprus Place and a start has been made on boarding up properties in preparation for their demolition and replacement by new residential properties. The side road which is visible, Livingston Street, has also vanished. However, the distant building with tower and flag pole behind the bus is still extant. It was the Ferndale pub which closed in 2006 and has been converted into upper floor residential units with a supermarket (now closed) on the ground floor. Route 101 ran from North Woolwich to Wanstead when this picture was taken in August 1980 but in this case the bus is working a short to Manor Park station. The service was crew-operated until 4 September 1982 and from 2005 has been diverted away from North Woolwich to Gallions Reach shopping park. RML 2494 was withdrawn in October 2005 and has been preserved. (Mike Russell)

During the 1970s and early 1980s the author undertook some part-time driving for Continental Pioneer of Richmond. On one occasion in October 1981, Pioneer was asked to provide reserve bus replacement services at Putney Bridge station during engineering work on the District Line and the author was allocated one of Ted Brakell's ex-Northern General (NG) Routemasters for this duty. NG had fifty of these long vehicles with front entrance doors, together with London prototype RMF 1254, and withdrew them in 1977-80. LT bought two for spares and twelve for possible use, numbering them RMF 2761-2772, but never operated them. The bus seen here was hired, along with another, to LT for the sightseeing tour and was designated RMF 2762 but renumbered RMF 2792 following the LT acquisitions. Brakell changed the livery from LT red to Lincoln green in 1980. The buses are parked near the bus stands in Gonville Street, having entered via Fulham High Street. The buildings are still in situ, the ICL block in Putney Bridge Approach having since been vacated by the famous computer company which itself no longer exists. (Author)

During the 1920s several independent operators introduced express services from the Home Counties into central London. One such operator was Amalgamated Omnibus Services and Supplies, trading as Batten's Luxurious Coaches, which ran services from Tilbury and Grays into London, latterly with the assistance of LGOC. These services were taken over by LT in December 1933 and numbered Green Line routes Z1 and Z2, becoming the 723 in 1946. Originally terminating at Aldgate (Minories) the service was extended to Victoria on 22 August 1981, which is the destination of SNB 225 in this view from March 1982 in Tower Hill. This bus is a far cry from vehicles such as the comfortable coach Routemasters that used to operate the 723. The service was eventually abandoned on 29 June 1991. The bus is about to pass the Mercantile Marine First World War Memorial completed in 1928. Between that structure and the bus, a section of the Roman London City Wall is visible. The lower part of the wall dates from c200AD. (R C Riley/Online Transport Archive)

RM 1934 prepares to turn from Gracechurch Street into Eastcheap in order to cross London Bridge on its way from Clapton Pond to Clapham Common in September 1982. Behind the photographer is the Monument built to commemorate the Great Fire of London which started nearby in 1666. The origin of route 35 can be traced back to 1906 when the Great Eastern London Omnibus Company operated a service between Epping Forest and Elephant & Castle. The LGOC took over the route in 1911 and numbered it 35. Routemasters were introduced onto the 35 in 1968 and these were replaced by OPO Titans on 21 June 1986. RM 1934 was sold for scrap at the end of the following year. The buildings in this scene are still standing except the one behind the right hand no entry sign. The ornate railings on the extreme left surround one of the first underground lavatories in London providing facilities for women as well as men and remains open. (R C Riley/ Online Transport Archive)

Green AN and red DMS buses vie for the photographer's attention in this scene outside the entrance to the Whitgift Centre, Wellesley Road, Croydon, in May 1981. Waiting at the bus stop on a 403 service is LCBS Leyland Atlantean AN 184, the first of a batch bodied by Roe due to the LCBS order being too large for Park Royal to fulfil in its entirety. AN184 entered service at Chelsham in January 1979 and was sold for further service in July 1998, ending up as a playbus in 2011. Pulling round AN 184 is DMS 1170 on route 64 which entered service in October 1975 and spent two years at Thornton Heath before being withdrawn in June 1982 and sold for further use. Behind DMS 1170 is MCW-bodied AN 119 on route 409 which entered service in November 1972 and was sold in May 1988. Bringing up the rear is DMS 61 on a 154 service which clocked up eleven years of service before being withdrawn in February 1982. (Chris Evans)

Opposite top: Route 237 (originally Hounslow garage to Chertsey) was introduced on 3 October 1934 due to its predecessor, the 137, being a single-deck service, thereby requiring to be renumbered in the 2xx series. The route was also OPO with old type Dennis Darts and did not become crew operated until 7 December 1942. It returned to being OPO on 27 January 1965 with RFs until RMs took over on 28 January 1978. It became OPO for the third and final time on 7 February 1987. RM 1067 in the foreground was based at Hounslow garage from August 1978 to August 1983 (two months after this picture was taken) and was withdrawn in December 1986 after which it made a one-way journey to Sri Lanka. This view of Chiswick High Road, at its junction with Chiswick Lane, has not significantly changed over the years and large trees are still in abundance. The wooden benches have been replaced by a single metal bench. (Edward Shepherd/London Bus Museum)

Above: Green Line coaches are monopolising Eccleston Bridge, Victoria, in this scene from August 1984. This was two years before the break up of LCBS into four divisions prior to being sold-off. Prior to this Green Line services had been enjoying a temporary fillip following the introduction of reliable, modern coach types such as these pictured here. In the foreground is TL 5, an ECW-bodied Leyland Tiger B51 in Flightline 757 livery. This Green Line service to Luton Airport still runs, operated by Arriva. Behind TL5 is an unidentified RB (AEC Reliance with Duple Dominant bodywork) belonging to the first generation of proper coaches for Green Line services. A very similar AEC Reliance, but with a Plaxton Supreme body, RS 116, is in the background on a 748 service to Northchurch, a village between Berkhamsted and Tring (Green Line route 748 also still operates). Finally, on the right and picking up passengers is DL11 (a Leyland Leopard with Duple Dominant bodywork) destined for Windsor on a 718. These coaches were all withdrawn after five or six years service, not because they were unsatisfactory but because their leases had expired. (Chris Evans)

Left: LT ceased operating the Round London Sightseeing Tour in 1983 because the market was required to be open to competition. Several sightseeing tour companies grasped this opportunity, most of which were short-lived because Ensigns cornered the market with a ready fleet of ex- LT buses. One such private company was Culture Bus of Feltham which entered the market in 1983 offering a hop-on, hop-off facility at any of twenty stops. The company sold out to Ensign two years later. This view from July 1984 at Hyde Park Corner depicts CB 5 carrying the name Ebenezer Scrooge below the windscreen. This Daimler Fleetline was originally LT's Park Royal-bodied DMS 576 from 1973. It was sold for scrap in April 1985, a year or so before the bus behind, Battersea-based RM 814 operating on route 22, met the same fate. (Alan Murray)

Metrobus M 261 travels through the slush in Southfield Road, Chiswick, heading towards Turnham Green on 20 January 1985. The E3 service formed part of the changeover to flat fare OPO working introduced in the Ealing area on 30 November 1968 and covered part of the former RT-operated 55 route. Over the years the E3 has fluctuated between double deck and single deck operation. Metrobuses replaced Leyland National LNs in 1981 and were in turn superseded by RW midibuses in 1990. The route has subsequently reverted to double deck operation. The E3 continues to serve Southfield Road today and this scene is virtually unchanged, even down to the privet hedge on the right. The bus stops refer now to Rugby Road which is a turning on the right on the bend in the background. (Charles Roberts)

The picture below bears witness to the unusual sight of a front-engined, crew-operated modern bus operating in London in Spring 1985. Alexander-bodied Volvo Ailsa demonstrator V 3 was the third prototype on trial but differed from V 1 and V2 by having two staircases and a second door near the rear which was out of the driver's sight, thereby requiring a conductor. LT then purchased a further sixty-two second hand with a similar configuration to the first two. V 3 was withdrawn in August 1992 after being impaled on a tree and has since been preserved. The vehicle is standing in Trafalgar Square outside Canada House and the six flags flying are those of Canadian provinces (from left to right: North West Territories, Newfoundland & Labrador, Saskatchewan, British Columbia, New Brunswick and Quebec). Behind the RM is 66 Trafalgar Square built for the Union Bank in 1871 and Grade II Listed, next to which, with the clock tower, is the former Canadian Pacific Railway Company building, now converted into apartments and called 1 Trafalgar Square. (Roy Marshall/ The Bus Archive)

With effect from 27 October 1985 the 56 service was altered to travel between Stepney East and Aldgate via The Highway instead of Commercial Road. However, T 579 is seen in the previous month diverted on to its prospective new routeing. The bus has just passed under the Fenchurch Street-Southend railway arches at Stepney East station (renamed Limehouse in 1987 when the DLR opened) and a new bridge has since been built in front of the old one carrying the DLR platforms. Route 56 was introduced on 21 June 1980 to serve the new Docklands development and the initial DMS vehicles were replaced by Leyland Titans from 18 April 1982. Poplar garage provided the buses until 27 October 1984 when operations were transferred to West Ham. The service was withdrawn on 21 November 1987, having been replaced by the DLR. T 579 entered service in September 1982 and was sold in 1999. As regards picture location, the vehicle is travelling along Branch Road (A101) and the temporarily closed road on the left is Ratcliff Lane. The buildings in the background form an early 19th century terrace (582-588 Commercial Road) and are Grade II Listed. (Edward Shepherd/London Bus Museum)

Above: Chigwell station on the Central Line of the Underground is served by Eastern National 1803, a Leyland National delivered to the Company in June 1977, in this view of LT route 206 in June 1986. Today there is no bus stop outside the station and the stop designated Chigwell station is considerably further along the High Street. Several routes currently serve this stop but not the 206 (Walthamstow to Chigwell) which was withdrawn on 4 March 1989 after being replaced by the W14 and W15. The 206 (not the Kingston one) had been a new route created on 31 January 1981 to replace part of the 235 (not the Richmond one, which the author sometimes drove). On 24 May 1986, operation of the 206 was transferred to Eastern National which almost immediately underwent considerable restructuring. It was privatised in October 1986, sold to Badgerline in 1990 and split into two divisions (North Essex and Thamesway). Badgerline then became a subsidiary of First Group and the two divisions were remerged and called First Essex in 1995. The station building has at least been subject to less change. It was constructed for the Great Eastern Railway in 1903 and taken over by LT when the Central line was extended in 1948. (Capital Transport)

Opposite top: Orpington was chosen as a guinea pig for a midibus network in the mid-1980s. A subsidiary of London Buses, Orpington Buses trading as Roundabout, commenced operation on 16 June 1986 of new route R1 (Bromley Common-Green Street Green – St Pauls Cray – Sidcup) using Iveco Daily (classified RH) 21-seater vehicles. These replaced Titans on Route 229 and unsurprisingly were found to be too small for the increasing travelling clientele. Two years later the RHs were replaced by MRLs and the provision of larger vehicles for the R group of routes has continued. The buses in this picture, photographed in September 1986 in High Street, Orpington at what is now bus stop S, are RH 17 christened Snipe and behind is RH 9 Heron. This bus was sold to Luton & District in May 1993 and ended up in Ireland in October 1995. RH 17 was transferred to Bexleybus in January 1988. This part of High Street is largely unchanged. The empty retail premises on the extreme right are now occupied by McDonalds. (Capital Transport)

Opposite: Metrobus of Orpington began operating in July 1983 and started with three routes, one of which was the 357 (Croydon-Orpington) which lasted until 1995. The Company was purchased by the Go-Ahead group in September 1999 although Metrobus branding is still used. The initial livery of Metrobus vehicles was mainly blue, as worn here by this Northern Counties- bodied Daimler Fleetline acting as a mobile advertising hoarding. The bus originated in 1972 as West Riding 709 until sold in 1984. This 1986 picture was taken as the Fleetline makes its way along High Street, Orpington. The parade of shops remains in situ, but occupied by different retailers. Martins, in the foreground, has become the Fab House Cafe at 260A High Street. (Charles Roberts)

In a setting unchanged today LS 181 leaves Blackheath Village for Lewisham on 3 July 1986, photographed from the Bennett Park road junction. The bus is carrying the striking Docklands Clipper livery applied to a handful of Leyland Nationals. These were for use on the new D1 route introduced on 3 January 1984 which ran from Mile End to the Isle of Dogs and formed part of the Enterprise Zone initiative for redeveloping London Docks. This short-lived service ran until 2 March 1989. The allotted buses were transferred from West Ham to Bow garage on 21 June 1986 but in this view LS 181 has strayed onto the 108 Stratford-Lewisham service. This route was later extended from Stratford to Wanstead and over subsequent years has been worked by buses in non-red liveries such as those of Kentish Bus and Harris Bus but is now operated by red buses again. (Alan Mortimer)

In treacherous weather conditions D 2631 travels gingerly along Chipstead Valley Road beside the Primary School (out of shot on the left). The bus is approaching the junction with Gidd Hill, Coulsdon, on its way to South Croydon garage on route 166 (Beckenham Junction – Chipstead Valley). The route has since been extended westwards to Banstead and Epsom but cut back eastwards to West Croydon. This picture was taken on 13 January 1987 at 1.15pm, the previous service from Chipstead Valley having been at 8.30am. The following two services were at 3pm and 6pm but, given the snow, passengers were lucky to have any buses running. The reign of DMS buses was however about to end because they were replaced on this service by Leyland Nationals (LSs) on 7 February 1987. Route 166 had started on 7 April 1948 and RTs, successors to the initial STLs, were replaced by OPO Swifts on 31 October 1970. Conversion to DMS operation took place on 6 January 1973. D 2631 entered service in August 1978 (as DM 2631) and was sold for scrap in June 1991. (Chris Evans)

This gathering of Routemasters at Victoria was probably photographed in the mid 1980s because the Gillingham Street (Victoria) based bus (RM 722) on the left working on route 11 and which has just emerged from Wilton Road was withdrawn in July 1986. The other identifiable bus is RM 1186 on another 11 service which was also allocated to Gillingham Street at around this time and was withdrawn at that garage in July 1993. Victoria bus station has undergone various transformations over the years but the three Grade II listed buildings (one is actually Grade II*) in this view have remained largely unaltered. On the extreme left is part of the 1909 section of the South Eastern & Chatham Railway station built in white Portland Stone, in the centre is the huge London, Brighton & South Coast Railway edifice from 1908 and to its right the Grosvenor Hotel from 1860 which is joined to the main station building by a bridge. (Martin Jenkins)

Probably taken at the same time as the previous picture, six Routemasters are at rest, have taken over the bus stands in the one-way section of Vauxhall Bridge Road, Victoria. The Apollo Victoria theatre on the left opened in 1930 and has twin entrances, the second being in Wilton Road which is one-way in the opposite direction. The light-coloured building in the distance is the Victoria Palace theatre but the building to its left has been replaced by an enormous glass slab on the corner of Victoria Street. Two of the buses are identifiable, RM 1162 on the 11 and RM 1240 on the 36. (Martin Jenkins)

Kingston introduced three Midi-bus routes in June 1987, numbering them K1-3 which is when this vehicle, MR 13, entered service under the Westlink Hopper branding. The K3 service, which was the former 215 re-numbered from 27 June 1987, ran initially from Kingston Cromwell Road to Esher and was extended eastwards to Kingston Hospital on 28 August 1993 and then to Roehampton Vale on 5 May 2001. MR 13 was a MCW Metrorider but these buses did not last long on the K3, being replaced by the larger MRL type on 24 September 1988. MR 13 was then reallocated but was withdrawn in July 1992 and sold for further use. In this view from February 1988, MR 13 has left the stand near the Bear in Esher and is proceeding along Claremont Lane, soon to turn into Milbourne Lane and head towards Claygate and Hinchley Wood on its way back to Kingston.   (Alan Murray)

It is the 1988 Boat Race in April (Oxford won!) and three Routemasters join the queue of traffic in The Terrace, while crowds line the pavement within the shadow of Barnes railway bridge. The buses are on their way to the terminus at Avondale Road, Mortlake. Until its closure in 1983, Mortlake garage would have been the destination shown on the blinds. The garage was located at the end of Avondale Road and has been replaced by a residential development and a tiny bus station used exclusively (apart from a schools service) by single deck route 209. This service replaced the Hammersmith – Mortlake end of the single deck 9A on 8 March 1997 which in turn had taken over this section of route 9 from 18 July 1992 because of a new weight restriction imposed on Hammersmith Bridge which banned heavy vehicles such as double deck buses. The location of this picture is unchanged today. (Richard Franklin)

This picture from June 1988 is remarkable for the absence of traffic in Park Lane allowing RML 2418 to have the road to itself. This bus, which is now a mobile catering vehicle in Liverpool, is lucky even to have lasted until 1988 because LCBS, which inherited it from LT in 1970 upon the transfer of the Country Area and Green line fleets, sold it to the well known Yorkshire scrapyard in March 1979. This was a time when LT was desperate to acquire Routemasters for its central London services from virtually any source because of the unreliability and unsuitability of many of its later types. On realising that LCBS was starting to sell its Routemaster fleet for scrap, LT quickly purchased RML 2418 in June 1979 and, after overhauling and painting it red, returned the bus to service at Highgate in December 1980. It was eventually withdrawn in September 2004. The location of this shot is the lower end of Park Lane. The small building behind the bus stops is now sandwiched between new developments. (Martin Jenkins)

This is route branded RML 2701 at Hyde Park Corner in June 1988, several years after it lost its all-over tartan livery (see page 63). The Jesus Army bus is one of a total of 662 Scania Metropolitans with MCW bodywork built. These had short lives due to excessive corrosion. LT purchased 164 which were delivered in 1975-77 and all were withdrawn by 1983. However, this particular example, WKH 423S, was one of thirty which Hull Corporation bought in 1975-78. It was Hull No 423 delivered in January 1978. The vehicle is passing the Grand Entrance to Hyde Park (also known as Apsley Gate) with three carriage entrance archways. It was completed in 1825. (Martin Jenkins)

On I November 1987 London Buses won the tender to operate Surrey County Council Sunday route 508 (Sutton-Banstead-Epsom) and this photograph shows a working in Bolters Lane, Banstead, in August 1988. The bus, D 2622, looks immaculate following a repaint in the previous month and in this view shows a total absence of logos, advertising or anything to indicate to whom it belongs. In fact, it was not until November that it received a mushroom-coloured skirt, Sutton Bus markings, a raised front number plate and a London Buses roundel with yellow bar. DM 2622 entered service in June 1978 and, as a dual-purpose D, remained in use until November 1991 when it then went into store and was sold for scrap. This location near the junction with Castleton Drive (behind the bus) is unchanged apart from the removal of the nearest tree and the installation of a separate bus stop carrying the LT style flag. (Alan Murray)

Although DMS 2343 appears to be travelling along a normal residential road (Sutton Lane), it is actually opposite Sutton garage. The road marked by white lines in the foreground is Bushey Road and the house behind the bus is also in Bushey Road. The apparent "dog leg" seems to have been created by the positioning of the former LGOC bus garage which opened in January 1924. DMS 2343 entered service in April 1978 and spent from October 1982 to February 1992 at Sutton garage before being withdrawn and sold for scrap. In this photograph taken in March 1989 the bus is carrying Sutton Bus markings and is operating on route 80 which, back in 1934, operated from Morden to Lower Kingswood and now covers Hackbridge to Belmont Prisons. This former RT service was converted to OPO RFs on 22 March 1969. These were succeeded by BLs in June 1976 and DMS Fleetlines took over Mon-Sat journeys on 25 April 1981, having operated on Sundays from November 1979. (Alan Murray)

Opposite: Chaos ensues in North End, Croydon, on 9 May 1989 following a serious accident which blocked the road. DMS 2431 on a 194B service stands at the back of a line of buses waiting to reverse onto the pavement which was busy with shoppers in order to turn back. At this time road traffic in North End was restricted to buses and delivery vehicles and not long afterwards it was pedestrianised. All but two of the buses have had their red livery augmented by grey skirts although DMS 2431 is yet to gain the London Buses roundel. This B20 entered service in June 1977 and spent most of its fifteen year career at Thornton Heath before being sold for scrap in June 1992. Route 194B (Shrublands Estate-Thornton Heath) operated from 27 February 1963 until replaced by the 198 on 14 March 1992. DMS buses superseded RTs and RMs on this service on 1 December 1973. The two buses nearest the camera are standing outside Woolworths. The flags in the distance are fluttering from the roof of Allders department store. Both retailers have subsequently became high street casualties. The tower in the distance belongs to the surviving Town Hall clocktower built in 1895. The lower picture depicts D 2642 in the process of turning round. (Chris Evans - both)

Above: From 1988 to 2008 the residents of Eltham, Sidcup and Swanley had to become accustomed to buses on route 233 arriving in a variety of colours other than red. The departure from red livery started on 16 January 1988 when Boro'line, a company owned by Maidstone Council, was awarded route 233. This photograph dating from August 1988 was taken in Station Road, Sidcup, with the Telephone Exchange on the right. The cross on the roof of the former Congregational church (built 1888) is just visible above the trees in the background. Boro'line collapsed in February 1992 and was bought by Kentish Bus. The double-decker, an Alexander-bodied Volvo B10M Citybus (Boro'line 764), was the last Volvo chassis built at their Irvine factory. It was initially used as a Demonstrator and was then earmarked for Fife Scottish before being bought by Boro'line, along with two other buses, to replace an order for Olympians cancelled due to delivery delays. In this view there seems to be a problem in fitting the front blind into the Scottish-style aperture. (Alan Murray)

The branding is grey-green but that livery, which latterly had been white-green anyway, has changed to white-orange in this picture taken in Mutton Lane, Potters Bar in August 1989. The bus is Grey Green No 465, a former South Yorkshire PTE MCW Metrobus dating from 1980 which was later owned by London Pride and converted to part open top. It served with a number of companies operating sightseeing services until it was scrapped in 2007. Grey-Green was acquired by the Cowie Group in 1980 and began to operate London bus routes in February 1987. Cowie Group rebranded itself Arriva in November 1997. This iteration of the 313 running from Potters Bar to Chingford commenced on 4 September 1982, succeeding a previous version which operated from Enfield to St Albans. Grey Green took over the route from London Buses on 22 February 1988 until 2 November 1996 when it passed to Leaside Buses, another Cowie subsidiary. (Alan Murray)

A procession of buses travel along Wellesley Road, Croydon, in September 1989 led by London & Country Leyland National SNB 331. It is wearing the striking livery of two-tone green with red banding which was introduced earlier in the year when the new trading name was adopted by the Drawlane group following its acquisition in February 1988 of London Country South West under privatisation. SNB 331 is working a 405 service from Croydon to Crawley which has since been cut back to Redhill and is now a TfL route with red buses. The vehicle was new in November 1977 and was sold for further work in November 1999 before being bought for preservation in April 2011. This bus is followed by DMS 2281 on route 109, behind which are more buses including an unidentified Leyland Olympian (LR) on a 197 service. The Leyland National is passing the junction with Bedford Park against the backdrop of two "modern" buildings which have since been demolished and replaced by a structure on stilts. (Chris Evans)

Six of the former BEA/British Airways fleet of sixty-five front-entrance Routemasters bought by LT were converted for "The Original London Transport Sightseeing Tour" in 1986, the work including the fitting of a blind box at the front. This picture taken in March 1990 depicts the final member of the class, RMA 65 (formerly BEA 65). The RMAs' last season on the Sightseeing Tour was 1993, whereupon RMA 65 was sold. It formed part of the "Peace Envoy" to Baghdad in 2003 and returned to the UK for further use. The bus is passing the Palace of Westminster (Houses of Parliament) and in the centre background the Victoria Tower and one of the four clock faces is visible. The structure is colloquially known as Big Ben which actually refers to the largest of the five bells contained within. (Chris Evans)

Studies in the late 1980s indicated that if bus frequencies were increased in conjunction with the use of small OPO vehicles passenger numbers would rise. This was on the basis that passengers were deterred from using buses through having to wait too long at stops whereas if buses came more often passengers would not mind what type of vehicle carried them. Routes 28 and 31 were chosen to inaugurate this policy and for the latter service 25 Alexander-bodied Mercedes Benz 811D midi-buses (classified MA) with 28 seats replaced 16 RMs with 64 seats from 15 April 1989. Passenger numbers did increase but so did complaints about overcrowding until larger buses were provided. In this view from May 1990 MA 58 is turning from Kensington Mall into Kensington Church Street. The bus was withdrawn in December 1997 and moved to Scotland for further work until it was sold for scrap in January 2003. Nowadays, this scene is largely unchanged. The flower bed remains in place overlooked by an attractive period lamp standard but the low-level buildings on the offside of the bus have been replaced. (Capital Transport)

Bus operation was complicated in parts of south west London in the 1980s and 90s as evidenced here with route 600. Tellings Golden Miller's routes 601 and 603 were transferred to Fountain Coaches in October 1985 and these services were combined into route 600 (Bedfont-Feltham-Hanworth) in June 1986. Fountain Coaches ceased trading on 7 April 1990 and on that date the 600 passed to Stanwell Bus trading as Westlink. This subsidiary of London Buses was privatised in 1994 and became part of London United in the following year. Meanwhile, route 600 was replaced by the H24 and H25 on 29 September 1990. In this photograph taken some three weeks before the 600 ended, LS 408, displaying an uninformative blind, is pulling into the bus stop in High Street, Feltham, outside the building called New Chapel Square. In the background is the spire of St Catherine's church. This closed in 1975 and was demolished but the spire, dating from 1898, remains and is attached to an office block. LS 408 was withdrawn in December 1997 and sold, becoming a mobile workshop. (Alan Murray)

In 1990 London Buses bought 90 Wright-bodied Renault S75 midi-buses (RW 1-90), many of which were allocated to the new E-Line services in the Ealing/Southall area. These included the E6 (Hayes station – Greenford station) which commenced on 21 July 1990. RW 15 entered service in March 1990 and is seen at Greenford Broadway in the following September. London's demanding traffic conditions soon caused the RWs to wear out mechanically and RW 15 was transferred to First's Bee Line operation (Berks and Bucks Bus Co) in July 1996, ending up with First Manchester in November 1999. In this picture, RW 15 is terminating at Greenford Red Lion, requiring the vehicle to turn from The Broadway into Greenford Road and then loop round into the bus stands in Windmill Lane. The landmark Red Lion pub stood on the opposite corner to Lavells, to the left of the picture, and was demolished in 2012. All the buildings seen here are still standing and the market stalls also remain. (Alan Murray)

This is no ordinary Metrobus but one of two Mk 2s which were delivered, along with sample vehicles from other manufacturers, to be evaluated in order to find the most suitable type to succeed the Titans and standard Metrobuses. M 1441, which has since been preserved, is seen here in September 1991 in Kennington Road and certain front-end differences between this and the remainder of the Ms (apart from identical M 1442) are visible. M 1441 entered service in August 1984 and is working route 109 which was a bus replacement service for tram routes 16 and 18 introduced on 8 April 1951. In the background is Lambeth North station, opened by the Baker Street and Waterloo Railway (the Bakerloo Line) in 1906. The station, a typical Leslie Green design with ox-blood red glazed faience cladding, was initially named Kennington Road until this was quickly changed to Westminster Bridge Road (its actual location) and finally to Lambeth North. The ecclesiastic building is the Lincoln Tower, commemorating Abraham Lincoln, dating from 1876 and is the only part of the former Christ Church Chapel complex to have survived bombing in the Second World War. (Capital Transport)

Regenerated Docklands provides the backdrop for this photograph taken in November 1990 in East Ferry Road at the junction with Selsdon Way. Immediately behind the bus is the DLR's Crossharbour station and in the distance finishing touches are being made to One Canada Square, unofficially called Canary Wharf. This edifice was completed in August 1991 and was Britain's tallest building until 2012. Approaching the cameraman is West Ham's Leyland National LS 88 in East London livery. This vehicle entered service in June 1977 and was transferred to Westlink in March 1992. Withdrawal came in 1998 whereupon LS 88 was sold and converted into a catering vehicle and then a control centre. In this view the bus is working a D5 service from the Isle of Dogs (Asda) to Mile End station. This route began on 4 March 1989 and finished on 17 September 1999. (Charles Roberts)

The C3 was a new route introduced on 13 April 1987 and after a few years Optare MetroRider midi-buses were assigned to the service as seen here in December 1992 when it operated between Earls Court and Clapham Junction. The service has since undergone several changes in routeing, operators and bus types over the years and the provision of larger vehicles has culminated in the use of double deckers from 6 May 2006. The bus shown here in Earls Court Road is MRL 199 which entered service in August 1991 and was sold in January 1999. It is seen passing Earls Court underground station, with its street building dating from 1906 which still carries its original legend: Great Northern, Piccadilly and Brompton Railway. When this tube line opened in 1906 it ran from Hammersmith to Finsbury Park and now forms part of the Piccadilly Line. Since this picture was taken, a blue "Tardis" style police call box has been erected on the pavement outside the station building although it is apparently no longer operational. Otherwise, this view has barely altered over time. (Charles Roberts)

DAF Optare Spectra SP 7 meets Volvo B10M-50 VC 28 in Brixton Road, Kennington in the summer of 1993 but SP 7 in particular had a short career in London. There were twenty five members of the SP class but whereas SP2 was a pre-production double-door bus, the remainder were single door vehicles. SP 7 entered service in December 1992 and was transferred away from London in July 2000 before being subsequently sold. SPs took over from Routemasters on route 3 when OPO was introduced on 2 January 1993. Stockwell-based VC 28 was one of 39 Volvo Citybuses and entered service in June 1990. It was sold in April 2002. The buildings seen here are all still standing but the cigarette advertisement above the front of SP 7 has faded slightly more. On the extreme right of the picture is the junction with Prima Road. (Geoff Morant)

Although the route number 23 had been around for a long time it was discontinued in 1985 but reused from 18 July 1992 on the service shown here, using RMLs. These were replaced on 15 November 2003 when route 23 became OPO and RML 2672 was withdrawn a few months later. The bus is now the Red Bus travelling fish and chip shop based in Lincolnshire. This photograph was taken on 20 June 1994 as RML 2672 turned out of Edgware Road into Sussex Gardens. All the buildings are still standing including the old one painted white which stands on the corner of Crawford Place. All the shops visible in this scene have changed hands over the intervening years apart from McDonald's in the distance. (Capital Transport)

Against the backdrop of the Cumberland Hotel (now the Hard Rock Hotel) built in 1929, with part of its Oxford Street facade incorporating the entrance to Marble Arch tube station, Leyland Titan T 478 from Upton Park garage turns to negotiate the Marble Arch roundabout. The bus is making its way from East Ham to Paddington on a 15 service in the early 1990s. In the background another Titan, T 502, heads down Oxford Street on route 10 which had been a new route introduced in 1988 to replace part of the 73. Both the 10 and 15 services were normally Routemaster-operated at this time except on Sundays when OPO Ts were provided. T 478 is carrying London Buses' East London branding which preceded the takeover by Stagecoach in October 1994. The vehicle had entered service in June 1982 and was withdrawn in December 1996, after which it was sold for further use. (Capital Transport)

Oxford Street in the 1990s was filled with Routemasters as this picture taken in June 1994 clearly illustrates. There are ten buses visible and eight of them are members of the RM family. At the front of the line is RML 2666, since preserved, working a 73 service from Stoke Newington. The 73 started life in 1914 running between Kings Cross and Barnes and was extended to Stoke Newington (and to Richmond) in 1935. Its western terminus has now been cut back to Oxford Circus. Bendy buses replaced RMLs on this route on 4 September 2004. The 13 clung on to its Routemasters until 22 October 2005 and in this view the vehicle is carrying the poppy red livery of BTS, the operator at this time. The vehicles are waiting at the traffic lights serving the junction with Orchard Street and North Audley Street. The first four blocks of buildings still survive as of course does Selfridges, out of view on the left. (Capital Transport)

Descending Ludgate Hill past the entrance to Pageantmaster Court in June 1994, Leyland Titan T 272 is heading for Waterloo on its journey from Hackney Wick on route 26. This version of the 26, about the tenth since 1911, was introduced on 18 July 1992 and brought the number back to Hackney Wick after some 77 years! T 272 was withdrawn in 1999 and sold for further use, before being despatched to a scrapyard in April 2007. On the left is RML 890 which, some six months later, was re-registered XFF 814 following acquisition on privatisation in September 1994 by Stagecoach East London. The bus was sold to Lord Andrew Lloyd Webber in March 2004 and still exists. So does the building in the background! This is St Paul's Cathedral, Sir Christopher Wren's masterpiece, which was officially completed in 1711 and replaced the previous St Paul's which was gutted during the Great Fire of London in 1666. (Capital Transport)

Open top buses were first introduced between Oxford Circus and Peckham (the origin of route 12) in 1850 under the auspices of Thomas Tilling and history is repeating itself here in September 1994 although the horses have been replaced! T 803 entered service in July 1983 and was converted to open top in December 1992, followed by the application of London Central Travel livery. It was later reclassified OT 803 and in June 2009 was sold to City Sightseeing in San Francisco. This photograph was taken at the lower end of Regent Street at the junction with Vigo Street and Glass House Street. On the right are the premises of Garrards, former jewellers to HM The Queen, with three Royal Coats of Arms hanging in the nearest window. The emporium is now occupied by a fashion retailer (106-112 Regent Street). The yellow road markings denoting a box junction have been removed but unfortunately so has the decorative lamp standard topped by three miniature crowns which was an appropriate adjunct to the royal warrants held by Garrards. (Capital Transport)

It would seem from this photograph that the heyday of the Routemaster was June 1996, forty years after the first RM entered service! Five of them are monopolising this part of New Oxford Street at its junction with Tottenham Court Road. Routes 73 and 38 remained in the care of RMLs until 4 September 2004 and 29 October 2005 respectively, replaced by articulated buses which only lasted a few years for various reasons. The two identifiable buses, both on the 38, are RML 2370 and, on the right, RML 2534. They seem to have been exported on withdrawal, the former to Australia and the latter to Canada. Here they are on their way to Clapton Pond although in the past the 38 had ventured out as far as Epping Forest. The skyscraper on the left of the picture is 34-storey Centre Point built in 1966. Much maligned for many years when it was an empty office block it is now regarded as a modernist masterpiece. Protected by English Heritage the building has just been transformed into very desirable residential units with stunning views over London. (Capital Transport)

In 1997 an edict was issued requiring all newly-tendered routes in central London to be operated by buses which were at least 80% red, with a few exceptions, eg historic liveries. The general view was that visitors to the Capital would expect the buses serving historic sites and tourist attractions to be red as they had been since the LGOC adopted this visibly strong colour for its fleet in 1911. The fact that non-red buses were operating a high-profile route, the 24, which passed the Houses of Parliament may have influenced the decision, though it was Margaret Thatcher who had insisted on the presence of private operators on London bus routes being very visible. The 24 is also considered to be the oldest unchanged service in London which has been running between Hampstead Heath and Pimlico since 1912. The livery problem is highlighted in this picture from March 1995 taken in Charing Cross Road near the junction with Great Newport Street and depicting some of the individual small shops which still dominate this area. As regards the vehicles, they are two Volvo B10-50 buses belonging to London & Country (No 655) and Grey-Green (No 125) in the colours of their owners while red Metrobus M 1314 lurks in the background. (Capital Transport)

A Leyland CU Cub belonging to Scorpio Coaches pulls out of Eastcote Lane into Northolt Road, South Harrow, in August 1995. This Duple-bodied midibus, formerly Lothian Buses No 160, entered service in November 1981 and is pictured here on route 398. This became a tendered LT service on 4 January 1997 when it was awarded to Sovereign Buses (a business later taken over by London United) but before 1997 it was independently operated by Scorpio Coaches (subsequently rebranded Blue & White) under an agreement with LT. This was a consequence of the overtime and rest day working ban in January/February 1966 which caused LT to withdraw several services and permitted private operators to run most of them temporarily. When the ban ended, LT reinstated the services apart from two, one being the Ruislip - Rayners Lane section of the 98B. Several operators tried to run a viable service until stability arrived in the form of Elmtree Transport. This Company accepted the challenge on 24 May 1971, operating the service until 22 January 1988. The routeing of the 98B was covered by new services H13 and 398, the latter operating between Ruislip and Northolt under the auspices of Scorpio. (Capital Transport)

When this picture was taken in June 1996 low floor buses were still a novelty, hence the initial branding to emphasise their status. By the end of 2005 the whole network had been converted to low floor operation and therefore wheelchair accessible, except the "heritage" sections of the 9 and 15. Route 101 was one of the first routes on which low floor single deckers were trialled in 1994, in this case using Wright-bodied Scania N113s. This example, SLW 22, belonged to a batch of sixteen for use by Stagecoach East on the 101 to replace high-floor Titans and entered service on 5 November 1994. They lasted on the 101 until superseded by Tridents in March 2006. SLW 22, renumbered 28622 in February 2003, was consigned to the scrapyard in August 2009 after some three years in use as a trainer. This scene is in High Street North, Manor House, at the Cranbourne Road bus stop just beyond the ecclesiastical-looking building which is Manor Park Community Centre. The junction with Romford Road is in the background on the left. (Capital Transport)

Although some of the places served have changed over the years route 31 has operated since 7 September 1911, initially between South Hampstead and Chelsea, replacing horse bus service 36. The Mercedes-Benz/Alexander MAs which had operated the 31 since 15 April 1989 were replaced by larger Dennis Dart/Wright 'Handy-bus' vehicles (the DW class) on 18 July 1992 and these lasted until superseded by larger Dennis Darts on 1 June 1998 and ultimately by double deckers. CentreWest operated the 31 using Gold Arrow branding as seen here on DW 121 in April 1997 although the company had been bought by First Group in the previous month. The bus is heading for Chelsea Worlds End (named after the district/the pub). The route now operates between Camden Town and White City. DW 121 was despatched from London to Norfolk in June 2000 and sold for scrap in July 2006. In this relatively unchanged scene the vehicle is turning from Kensington Church Street (opposite St Mary Abbots Church out of view on the left) into Kensington High Street. (Capital Transport)

RM 436 takes on passengers in the middle of Wilton Road outside the Apollo Victoria Theatre on 11 June 1997. This was the venue for the musical performed on roller skates, Starlight Express, which ran from 1984 to 2002. Routemasters were replaced on Route 36 by MDs on 13 April 1976 but Routemasters took over again on 31 January 1981. RMs were finally ousted on 29 January 2005 by OPO Plaxton Presidents (PVLs). The bus bearing the number RM 436 entered service in November 1960 and was withdrawn in January 2005, followed by exportation to Norway. When it operated on the last day of RMs on the 36 it had been re-registered 791 UXA. The bus standing in the shadows alongside Victoria Station (Kent side) is M572 which entered service in July 1981 and was sold for scrap in February 2001. (Capital Transport)

Pulling out of Station Road, Edgware into the A5 Edgware Road during August 1998 is this low floor Dennis Dart, DLD 30, a dual-door Plaxton Pointer. The vehicle entered service in October 1997 and was withdrawn from London service in 2008 after which it was used by various operators until sold for scrap in 2013. Route 32 was introduced on 13 June 1970, replacing part of the 142, and was operated by RMs for the initial nine months until conversion to OPO. It has remained a double deck route except for a four year period from 1996-2000. This scene is still recognisable today although the tower block looks completely different. The overhanging tree stands in the churchyard of St Margaret of Antioch. (Capital Transport)

This is a scene on 12 August 1998 at North Finchley which, at first glance, is now unrecognisable although all the buildings are still extant. The location is Nether Street, looking from Ballards Lane towards High Road in the background. This short section of Nether Street is pedestrianised and the bus station seen here, previously used by trams and trolleybuses, has been replaced by a high rise development which includes an indoor replacement bus station. The pub behind the buses is the former Cricketers which, when seen here, was called the Coach Stop. It has now been turned into a shop. A short distance away is the well known Tally Ho Corner and the Tally Ho pub at the junction of Ballards Lane and High Road. The bus nearest the camera is MCW Metrobus M 84 which entered service in October 1983 and was withdrawn by April 2001. Route 82 (Golders Green-Victoria) started on 21 June 1986 primarily replacing parts of the 2 and 2B. (Capital Transport)

George Street in Croydon as seen here in March 1999 looks very different now. Apart from the replacement of the buildings on the right, leaving just the two furthest on the left opposite East Croydon station, buses can no longer travel over tram tracks since Tramlink opened in May 2000. Indeed, in a reversal of historical practice, the X30 service worked here by Leyland Olympian L 232, ceased operation on 10 May 2000 and was replaced by trams. L 232 entered service in January 1987 and was withdrawn in July 2004 when it was sold to a Welsh operator. The bus in front on the 466 is L 197 which was sold in June 2005 and dismantled for spares. However, the Metrobus Volvo Olympian with East Lancs Pyoneer body, S850 DGX, is still at work. This entered service in September 1998 to operate route 119 and when it was sold to Bus Eireann in Cork, Ireland, in October 2004, it was converted into an open top bus for sightseeing numbered OT I (reg 98 C 24747). The destination shown here is Croydon Airport which closed in September 1959! Opposite its entrance on Purley Way was the Water Palace which is the real destination. However, this closed in 1996 and was replaced by The Colonnades Leisure Park. Blinds for the 119 now show The Colonnades rather than Croydon Airport. (Charles Roberts)